History of a Soft A'porth

Peter Benson

Copyright © 2021 Peter Benson
All rights reserved
ISBN- 9798538579051

II

This memoir is dedicated to my brilliant and beautiful wife Madeleine and my amazing and talented daughters Darcy and Remy.
Truly loved...

Contents

Introduction		P. VI
Prologue		P. VIII
Ch. 1.	Home	P. 1
Ch. 2.	Infants' School	P. 9
Ch. 3.	Fred	P. 14
Ch. 4.	Mr Taylor	P. 27
Ch. 5.	Secondary School and Other Animals	P. 34
Ch. 6.	Sweet Sixteen	P. 48
Ch. 7.	Sex 'n drugs 'n rock and roll?	P. 69
Ch. 8.	Academia	P. 90
Ch. 9.	Frodo	P. 102
Ch. 10.	Get a Job!	P. 109
Ch. 11.	Greasepaint: 1 – Foundation	P. 121
Ch. 12.	Snap!	P. 135
Ch. 13.	Dance the night away	P. 159
Ch. 14.	On the Hill	P. 175
Ch. 15.	Greasepaint: 2 – Age and Character	P. 187
Ch. 16.	Last Lines: A Mad World	P. 195

Introduction

I begin this in the middle of a global pandemic. Covid 19 is raging across the entire planet. Spread faster than the Black Death thanks to fast international transport connections, everywhere it is killing thousands of the elderly and vulnerable, and, inexplicably, thousands also of the seemingly fit and healthy. Mercifully, it seems to spare the very young, who usually – if they catch it at all – only suffer mild symptoms. The thought of it also taking our children would be too heavy to bear.

It was widely predicted by epidemiologists, and chillingly foreseen by film-makers, for example Steven Soderberg; plot elements of his prescient 2011 film *Contagion* could be the story of Covid 19.
Thankfully, at the time of writing, there is – as in *Contagion* – light at the end of the tunnel, with the deployment of various vaccines, but we cannot ever expect to return to the world as it was. Too much has changed.

We've all been touched by the virus in some way. Thankfully, most survive an infection, but even if we ourselves have not been ill, or lost a beloved family member or friend to this vile disease, we all know someone who has, and those who die sometimes do so isolated and afraid. These personal tragedies, along with the distancing measures in place, and the restrictions on contact and movement, make it feel like wartime... except, in wartime, people can at least bond together for mutual comfort and spontaneous entertainment. The virulent transmission of this disease denies us even that; not only are we scared, we are often alone and cheerless.

It is this fragmentation of the connections within our lives, and with those we hold precious, added to the fact that I have recently read the (excellent) memoir of a rediscovered friend, that has finally provoked me, after years of prevarication, to write my own. Fleeting though I know this story's interest will be, I find some of these events so moving, still, so compulsively relatable, in all senses of the word, that I can no longer resist sharing them.

So, with apologies to all those friends and families who've heard these stories before – some, many, many times – this is my life.

Peter Benson, July 2021

Prologue

I'm five and a half. It's dark when we get back. It's midsummer, and we've been away for a few days in Wales. Mummy pumps up and lights the paraffin lamp and the little primus stove, and puts on the kettle. She notices a pan she must have forgotten on the fireplace when we left.

"Oh bugger! the soup!"

She lifts the lid, and I'm at the same time fascinated and repulsed to see revealed a seething mass of what must be *dozens* of big fat cockroaches writhing like some multi-jointed beast, and almost filling the pan.
My mother slams the lid back on – how have they got in there? The lid must have been left slightly askew; the grotesque idea runs through my mind that they have conspired to prise it up sufficiently to effect entry.
The kettle boils. As its whistle dies away, my mother swiftly lifts the pan lid, pours in the scalding water in a hissing stream, and bangs the lid back down again.

Older, I've no recall of what subsequently happened to the broiled cockroaches; most of my childhood memories become fragmented with age, but that scene – that demonstration of life's ability to transfix, to entrance, to thrill, to engage wonder, and yet equally to despoil, to be shocking, to repel – will colour my perceptions forever.

History of a Daft A'porth

Chapter 1:   Home

On these magic shores children at play are for ever beaching their coracles. We too have been there; we can still hear the sound of the surf, though we shall land no more.

J.M. Barrie, Peter Pan

"You don't love me anymore!"
1955, my earliest memory. It's the end of the summer of my fourth year, and I'm kneeling on nannie's armchair with my head down in the cushion, screaming with rage because they have just told me I'm going to start school soon. Nannie (what I call my grandmother, not the other kind!), comforts me in her own way.
"Don't be daft, of course we love you. Everybody's got to go to school. It'll be lovely!"
I remain unconvinced, and continue my protests until worn out. As an only child, I have some leverage in the protest department – some, but sadly not enough to influence the outcome in this case.

My mother and I live with her parents Louis and Alice Hampson (my nannie and grandad) in a tiny two-up-two-down at 10 York Terrace, in the Boothtown area of Halifax. The two-up are my grandparents' bedroom and that of my mother and me; the two down are the living room and (Holy of Holies) the Front Room (indisputably capitalised). No bathroom; no kitchen; outside toilet in the small yard; cellar.
We cook on the small range in the living room, either on the coals, or in its small side oven. Toasted crumpets on the open fire are a particular treat.
Washing is done either in a tin bath in front of the fire, or down in the cellar, in the big stone sink with its massive tap. All hot water is laboriously boiled on the living room fire. In the cellar live also several wondrous items: the copper with its plunger, the washboard, and best of all, the mangle. This is our laundry,

where I pass foamy hours helping nannie or mummy to do the washing; plunging the plunger, turning the fairground-sized wheel on the mangle, squeezing the sopping clothes through its massive rollers, and chilling at the idea my fingers might follow them in. The memories are of warm steamy clouds, and lots of grey soapy water.

Paradoxically, this same cellar houses the coal bunker, down whose chute pours, every couple of weeks, a cascade of dusty black rocks. This I look forward to with great excitement; the arrival of the coalman, his cart horse-drawn and piled with filthy black sacks, which he hoists with straining biceps onto his back, carries, bent with the weight, into our yard, and decants down the coal hole in a thunderous cascade. Dust fills the cellar. The joy of this regular sooty landslide is offset by the tediousness of having to fill endless scuttles of the stuff, and cart it upstairs to the living room hearth – a task no-one in the family particularly enjoys, and which, four years old or not, sometimes falls to me.

Directly above the magical cellar is the (equally theatrical in its own way) Front Room. In common with many working-class families of this generation, we hold the Front Room in almost reverential esteem. It is unlike the living room, whose small space is crammed with two armchairs, a dining table with four chairs, an upright piano, and various small items of other furniture – always busy and warm, and never empty. The Front Room almost always is... empty, that is. Of people, certainly. It does contain chairs – two armchairs as in the living room – two or three dining chairs, a coffee table, and a couple of glass-fronted cabinets full of cheap cut-glass goblets and 'special' china (which I am occasionally allowed to touch.)

We use this room for Visitors (again the capital letter). They are allowed in here on Special Occasions, and drink sherry. They come – aunts, uncles, friends, members of clubs – and are ushered into the Front Room. In winter the electric fire in the hearth is put on, and glows orange, smelling strongly of burning dust. Drinks are served, and sandwiches and biscuits handed round. Nannie, plump, soft, and busy, in a severe high-collared black dress, presides, handing round the trays. Grandad with his

History of a Daft A'porth

long legs, shiny bald head, and pinkly shaved chin, settles his long thin frame into one of the armchairs, and supervises, teacup and saucer in hand.

They seem to me like a king and queen in a crowd of courtiers. I'm sometimes lucky enough to be included in the company, and even get the odd sip of sherry!

I'm also allowed sometimes to play here – especially if it's raining, and on these occasions, it's transformed into a palace of invention. The coffee table is upturned and sails across oceans, the armchairs loom, castle-like on the soft furry rug of their moat, and battles are fought for hoards of precious treasure in the towering, crystal-fronted caves.

I'm blessed with a vivid imagination, and these things come easily to me. I think I get it from my grandad.

Grandad was an entertainer. He's the one who plays the piano in the living room. He tries to get me to play, but I'm not interested in more than messing about tinkling randomly. I'd rather listen to him play. Oddly, my fragmented adult memory banks will have no record of his actual singing or playing, just the firm knowledge that he did.

What I *will* remember vividly is the Magic Book.

The Magic Book lives on a shelf above grandad's armchair. Both it and the shelf, although completely imaginary, are utterly real to me. They have size, shape, colour, and weight.

Most bedtimes, grandad sits me on his knee in the armchair, reaches his long elegant hands over his head to take down the Magic Book, and "reads" me a story. They come from some place inside his head, and are always entrancing, full of warriors, dragons, adventures, fairies, and everything you can find in the real books we also read. I am already an avid consumer of literature, both read to me, and as I learn, read by me. I'm thrilled listening to my first classic: Treasure Island, and from here on, thanks to my family's love of them, I will always adore books.

There's more to life than books, of course; I play out a lot. The narrow back-to-back streets surrounding us are almost completely traffic free, and there are plenty of other kids to play with. We tear up and down in the way children do, and in the small local park, just a street away, we fashion spears out of pampas grass, and kill each other over and over in the jungle of the park's herbaceous borders.

We're not posh enough to have a garden, but there is a tiny patch of grass outside the back of the house, in which grow various flowering things. One day, digging with nannie to plant one of these, I'm startled to see emerge a strange multi-legged and jointed bottle-green *thing*, that careers in what appears to be my direction. I scream and beat a hasty and apprehensive retreat, only to be ticked off by nannie with, "It's only a caterpillar, you soft ap'orth!" ("Ap'orth, being the diminutive of "ha'pennyworth"). I choose, nonetheless, to regard it as a relative of the creatures from my grandfather's Magic Book, and prefer to keep my distance.

Our patch of grass, the park, and the neighbouring gardens, all form a kind of green belt that surround our terrace, and stretch down to the scrubby valley below us. This valley is traversed by the thinnest and tallest iron foot-bridge ever to be built, across which my mother goes to work, and across which I occasionally venture with an adult (and later, on my own), gripped by anxiety at the precariousness of its structure. It seems to be a mere cast-iron thread supported on spindly, overstretched lamp-posts, with the slightest of railings along either edge. It's my first brush with real fear, but I face it.

My mother crosses the iron bridge daily to her job as a weaver at Crossley's carpets. A good job, apparently. My grandparents look after me while she's there. It's the biggest carpet manufacturer in the world, they tell me, and its massive mill buildings and tall chimneys dominate the town. There they make the famous Axminster and Wilton carpets, and send them all over the world. As will many of the UK's manufacturing centres, it will close down in the latter half of the century because of overseas competition, and the buildings will become small business and artisan workshops, but for now it clatters and wheezes importantly, and along with my mother, employs a substantial number of the local population.

History of a Daft A'porth

Nannie and grandad don't work. At least they don't appear to, to my four-year-old eyes. They're always here. Mummy works. Mummy works a lot, and I don't get her to myself during much of the day. But we do spend time together. Sometimes she plays with me in the front room, sometimes we go to the shop (It's a while before this term becomes the middle-class plural in my world); sometimes we do the laundry together, and she's always there to see me to bed. I don't get to sleep easily, and she is often summoned by my insistent "Mummy?" I occasionally wet the bed, and she has to deal with that, but thankfully that will not persist.

Of course, I'm sometimes ill, and she makes an effort to be there, especially when the doctor comes (yes, home visits!) On rare occasions we even have a special trip out. Like the works outing to Blackpool; hundreds of us crammed into a convoy of coaches hired by the firm for the day – and I get my first look at the sea. One summer we go to the Isle of Man, and I forge a lasting memory of climbing to the top of some kind of medieval tower, and feeling excitedly vertiginous. Maybe it's from this that I will find my later love of mountain tops?

Not all of our outings go so well. One of many to a tea shop, with 'aunty' Mary (all my mother's friends received the appellation 'Aunty' or 'Uncle') is occasion for me to be naughty, kicking aunty Mary's shins under the table, and receiving a slap from my mother across the legs for it. Perhaps my first? Certainly not the last. But she loves me, mummy; as do nannie and grandad.

I know this to be true, despite my head-down protestations in the armchair. I'm well treated compared to some of my peers, who are openly, and regularly, knocked around by their families. One or two are inclined to spread the pain of chastisement by taking it out on their mates. I receive my fair share of this, particularly from a boy called David, probably only a year or so older, but who has already developed the classic persona of the bully. At one point, he commandeers my little red pedal car, which I love dearly, and refuses to return it, until grandmotherly retribution intervenes. I get my little car back, but inevitably, there is payback later.

Peter Benson

Thankfully, none of this is serious. As tiny children we may be materially poor, and the world we inhabit constrained – the streets and alleys immediately neighbouring ours, the nearby park, and the gardens of neighbours lucky enough to have one – but we lead lives that are filled with adventure, and are generally joyful.

This world is mostly populated with our families and our neighbours of course, but there also regular visitors. These, although we only encounter them in the streets around our homes, are as familiar and accepted as friends or relatives. They form a kind of visiting extension to the tribe. There is the celebrated coalman, with his placid, big-eyed horse, to which we feed carrots and apples as he waits stolidly in the street; then, almost as regularly the rag and bone man, laboriously pulling his own cart. His "Any iron, brass, copper; anything to go?" stops occasionally when someone runs out of their house with a "Hang on a tick – here take this;" an old broken bucket or a pile of tatty clothing in hand, some bottles, or an old bedstead... whatever has passed its shelf-life even in these run-down make-do-and mend households.
But best of all amongst this regular crew, are the ice cream man and the pop man!
The ice cream man is announced – in these days before the electronic jingle of Mr Whippy – by a real bell; a traditional hand-held clanger-inside school-type bell, held out of the window by the non-driving hand, and shaken furiously at the beginning and end of each street. We plead, we beg, we implore our parents... "Please can I have an ice cream? Can I have a wafer?" (Wafers, though messier, and liable to over-squeezing, have a higher ratio of ice cream to biscuit!).
If successful – usually, it has to be said – we rush out and join the well-behaved, if noisy queue at the van, to return subsequently, licking the drips running down our hands from greedily grasped cornets, lollies, and wafers. On a good day, we

History of a Daft A'porth

get sprinkles or raspberry sauce, or even – what joy – that nirvana of the cryogenic dessert... a chocolate flake, sticking up like a wrinkled gatepost above the soft dome of ice-cream: the fabled '99.' The flake must be consumed as slowly as possible, used as a fragile spoon to scoop up luscious mouthfuls of ice cream in which fragments of its splintery chocolate are embedded. Rarely can life be better.

The pop man, although below the ice cream man in the hierarchy, comes close in the excitement generated by his appearance. Pop, of course, is fizzy drinks. His lorry lurches, rattling and clinking, into the street, laden with bottles of all sizes: half-pints, pints, quarts, and huge gallon-demijohns with their spring-wired tops. Orangeade, lemonade, cherryade, cream soda, etc. and best of all – the elixir of pop – dandelion and burdock. This is, long before the term will be coined by the consumer generation, the Marmite of the soft-drinks world. You either hate it, or as I do, adore it. With its slightly sour, slightly bitter, slightly sweet taste, nothing comes close. But imagine the heights of ecstasy we reach when presented with that pinnacle of gastronomy – when we are allowed a mixture of ice cream *and* pop! A real American-style soda, fizzing and foaming with outrageous luxury in a dessert bowl. If enough time and personal restraint allow, the whole subsides into a creamy, cold, bubbly soup, which can be drunk with sloppy bad manners from the edge of the bowl. Heaven!

The last of our demi-monde of regulars are the pig-men.

About half way along each of the streets where we live, there are little alleys that run perpendicular to, and join, the long streets. Within each of these alleys, serving half the row each, are two metal dustbins. Not used for the normal detritus of household life, these are the 'pig bins.' Long before the world will belatedly decide that it is vital to recycle as much as possible, these bins are temples to food waste. All our peelings: potato, orange, Bramley apple, onion, etc, bones, fat, stale bread, all foodstuffs beyond human consumption, go into these, to be taken to local farms 'for the pigs.' They're emptied weekly, by the 'pig-men.' We have 'dustmen' for the standard dustbins, and we have 'pig-men.' That's what they're called. They seem to take no offence at the name, and happily use it of themselves. This activity – collecting food waste – seems to be something they're proud of. Looking at it in the future, it will seem to me that they were way ahead of their time. There is, apparently, nothing new under the sun.

So we play: in our yards, in the park, in the streets. We chase happily after the ice cream man and the pig men on their rounds. Those of us lucky enough, have stories read to us, and go to tea with our aunties at Lyon's Tea Shop. We are happy; we are free. For a while...

History of a Daft A'porth

Chapter 2: Infants' school
   Wisdom begins in wonder
            Socrates

As an adult, I will visit the Louvre in Paris many times, on my own or – a particular joy – with each of my two daughters. On almost all of these occasions I follow a habitual path into the underground corridors of this vast French monument to art and history. It winds through remains of the original medieval walls of the chateau that stood on the spot centuries ago. The effect is impressive. Almost oppressive. The corridor through these walls is kept narrow – deliberately, I imagine – to increase the dominating aspect of the stones above, and one feels small and intimidated passing beneath them.

This feeling will reawaken, with uncanny accuracy, the sensation I have now as a child of four entering Boothtown infants' school, with its (to me) towering perimeter wall, the length of which we walk to the school office, and which will circumscribe my playtimes for some time to come.

The school itself is also massive! At least that's how it seems to me, dragged reluctantly into the playground desperately clutching mummy's hand on my first day. There are huge square blocks of buildings unlike anything I've seen before, completely dwarfing my home-gathered images of neat little terraced houses and the occasional shop. Different even from those buildings in the centre of town, which, though tall, possess that Victorian gentility, a soft-edged quality that welcomes you in for a cup of tea and a currant teacake, all decorative cornices, flutes, and columns. These school buildings are like nothing I have seen before, and appear more likely to bark sharply at one than to nod hello. It's all a bit scary. Inside is also square and hard everywhere, enlivened only by brightly coloured pastel paintings (I catch on that they must be done by the children), on the walls. Mummy says goodbye, and leaves me there. My earlier suspicions are at last confirmed; nobody loves me anymore!

But of course, it's not as bad as all that. I settle in without too much fuss. As most children are, I am swiftly taken up by the rhythm of school life. Memories of this place, though fragmentary, will be mostly happy ones. They include: The Climbing Frame, which we swarm up like chimpanzees, the Railings, which we traverse like Hillary and Tensing on the face of Everest, and The Tyre Pile. This, a huge heap of old car tyres in the playground, is the focus and factory for a myriad of adventures in the limitless lands of our imaginations. As can the humble cardboard box, a car tyre or two may assume a multitude of identities: sailing ship, space rocket, train, tunnel, or indeed, given sufficient momentum from the top of the sloping playground, a car tyre in rapid motion. And heaven help anyone in its way!

Vehicles feature large in our play. A favourite game is Trains. Our playground has a sports court of some type marked out on it for the older children, and we have adopted it as our rail network and goods yard. We chug along the lines like Thomas and his pals, hooting and hissing at junctions, our arms pistonning furiously. There are strict rules: If you approach someone head on, the one closest to his or her last-passed junction or corner must reverse. If they can turn off before meeting head-on, they must. Other rules abound, based sometimes quite arbitrarily on whoever is the more persuasive at the time. These rules are to be disregarded at one's peril: on one occasion, one of my classmates is carted off to the nurse's office with a bloody nose after an unfortunate encounter between two passenger expresses on the main line.

At break time, there is milk. Remarkable as it will seem to future generations, in 1955, when I begin school, all children up to the age of 18 are entitled to free milk every day. Secondary schools will lose it in 1966, and it will be withdrawn completely in the nineties. ("Thatcher, Thatcher – milk snatcher!") For us it is delivered to the school in one-third-of-a-pint-bottles every morning, and distributed at first break. Each of us gets a straw, which we plunge into the metal foil cap, and then retire to our tables to drink. The mere fact of this state largess is unusual enough, but what will be the most abiding aspect for me, is the

History of a Daft A'porth

difference a season or two can make to one's culinary appreciation. In winter and the colder months of spring and autumn, the milk, for those that like it – and there are some who don't – is a delight. Its arrival at the school is a cause for joy close to that for the ice cream man in our street. The milkman usually comes to our homes too early in the morning to be part of that elite brotherhood featuring the ice cream man and others, but at my school he is a well-known and popular chap. We surround his crate-rattling figure, jumping with excitement. Sometimes the milk is left in the playground for too long before it's brought inside, and begins to freeze. This magically fills every crate with a forest of snowy, solid cream stalagmites, each with its shiny foil hat at a rakish angle. If we're lucky, we get to eat these luscious extrusions off the tops of our bottles before drinking the deliciously cold milk beneath.

In summer, it's a different matter. Left in the playground or not, the milk attains an unpleasant tepid state that even the most avid lactophiles among us find difficult to stomach – literally – and many half-drunk bottles are returned to the crates. Sometimes it gets so much sun, that it reaches the temperature of slightly stale tea – and is even less palatable. Although I will continue always to enjoy a glass of chilled milk, the taste of it warm will forever evoke disgust in me, even in adulthood.

More immediately and painfully distressing, however, is The Splinter...

We have PT in the hall. It ranges from trying to pick up bean bags with your clenched toes to bunny jumps and forward rolls. We do these exercises on rubber mats on the wooden floor of the hall. One day, during one of the activities, I place my hands outside the mat on the floorboards, and as my left one slides forward, a large flat splinter rams itself under the nail of my middle finger.

It is excruciatingly painful, and of course I scream the place down. My hand is bandaged, and I have to go home; the idea of extracting the embedded villain is too horrific for me to contemplate.

At home, nannie is brusque.

"What you need is a poultice: soap and sugar." I've no idea what this means, but all is revealed as nannie takes a piece of gauze, smears onto it some softened green soap from the edge of a Fairy laundry bar, and rubs in a generous pinch from the sugar jar. This is wrapped around my injury, and secured with Elastoplast. "That'll bring it out." she assures.

Even at the age of four, I am, as we have seen, capable of scepticism, and not afraid to express it; which I do... with much whining.

"Don't mither! You'll see, it'll be right." Says nannie.

I have to wait two painful days, but I then witness a miracle. The bandage is removed, and there, sticking up above the curve of my finger, for all the world like one of my coveted flakes in a 99, is visible at least half of my assailant. Somehow, (and many times in later life, when I have acquired a modicum of science, I will try to figure out by exactly what mechanism), the poultice has magically caused the splinter to partially extrude itself from my nailbed. It sits there, pointedly suggesting that someone encourage it the rest of the way out.

Unsurprisingly, I'm not hugely in favour of this, and have to be physically restrained by both my grandparents as mummy takes a pair of tweezers to the offending item. I look away, and brace myself for the agony.

"There!" She waves the tweezers in front of my averted eyes.

"Is it out?"

"Of course it's out you daft 'a-porth; this's' it." She indicates the massive shard in the tip of the tweezers.

I'd not even felt it go. All that anticipation of pain, and out it came without a twinge. I will forever regard the miracle of my grandmother's soap-and-sugar poultice as rivalling any of the achievements of modern medicine, and I proudly boast of her mystic skills over and over again in the playground, for as long as my classmates will tolerate it.

These then, are my first forays into the world of school. Not much of the actual education I receive will remain at my recall. I learn to read and count (thanks to my grandparents, I could

History of a Daft A'porth

already do a little before school), and there must of course be many other lessons. What I will retain, however, are those pleasures and pains recounted above, which provide the major highlights and despairs of this period. It's a whole new world, and I throw myself enthusiastically into it. I've a secure and happy school, I still play out in the streets around 10 York Terrace, and mount expeditions into the jungles of the nearby park. I have mummy, nannie, and grandad at home, lots of friends, and a safe world to explore in my own little adventures. For me, all is stable and well with the world.

That's about to change.

Chapter 3: Fred

> They fuck you up, your mum and dad.
>   They may not mean to, but they do.
> They fill you with the faults they had
>   And add some extra, just for you.
>
> *Philip Larkin*
> *This Be the Verse*

I have up to now rarely heard mention of my father. I've picked up, from snatches of conversation, the fact that I have one somewhere, along with a whole other set of grandparents and family, none of whom I have ever met. All I can understand is that mummy and daddy don't live together, and that we don't mix with the other side of my family. It will be some time before I'm told the reason: that I was an accident. That my mother and father had married because I was on the way, after a relationship which, though for my mother was a serious one, wasn't seen as such by my father. Their 'doings' – as my grandmother put it – having resulted in pregnancy, and given the moral strictures of the period, a 'respectable' union was demanded. I don't know it yet, but I'm the tail end of the post-war baby boom... the eventually to be called 'Boomers,' and will benefit from, if not a golden, then at least in many ways a more gilded age than either my forebears or my children.

The marriage didn't last. Not only was it a shotgun wedding, they were totally unsuited. Although attractive and intelligent, my mother is very poorly educated – having left school at thirteen – and thoroughly and proudly working class. My father, I learn – a morsel of information at a time – is an electrical engineer, laying cables for such as the Post Office, and even abroad, and is lower middle class. Such is the rigidity of the class structure in these times, that they are socially and culturally a world apart. It became rapidly evident that apart from the physical attraction, there was nothing they had in common; so my mother left, taking me with her to live with her parents. Derrick, my father, I am told, is now working in Saudi Arabia – wherever that is!

My paternal grandparents live at the other end of the universe, in Cleckheaton, a small town near Bradford, and to all intents and purposes are too toffee-nosed to associate with us. Nonetheless, occasional visits are arranged (for me only), to stay with grandma and grandpa Clara and Percy Benson.

What a revelation! Clara and Percy are so very different to nannie and grandad. Percy goes regularly to church, and is a stalwart member of the choir and church community. Gruff-voiced, but gentle, he is a dapper old gent with a bushy mop of grey hair – unlike grandad Louis. Clara speaks with what I recognise as a Posh Voice, and is terribly elegant. In contrast to nannie, she is slim and petite, which she makes up for with an edge of severity in her cultured tones. In vivid contrast to ours, their house is neat and tidy. They have a proper kitchen, and an inside bathroom in which I take luxurious baths. As an infant, I'm rather curiously allowed the dubious indulgence of peeing whilst in the bath instead of having to get out and dried, then back in. A mixed blessing for those supervising, I imagine (Looking back, I can't remember or imagine how my final exiting of the bath was managed, but standards change!). They also have a small allotment just 'up the road a bit,' in which I help Percy mostly, to seed, dig and harvest, and to hammer nails into the little fence as I strain to hold an improvised brick-as-anvil on the other side.

Through Clara and Percy, it's arranged for me to visit my aunty Joan and uncle Bob's house, discovering there a cousin, Valerie. We two dig mighty holes in their garden, and Valerie almost renders me pirate-eyed during a game with home-made bow and arrow, as a shaft from her weapon lodges in my cheek about half an inch from my right eye, dangling there like a long wooden teardrop. Aunty Joan is incandescent with horror and fury at poor Valerie, who – a few years older than me – understands perfectly the extent of her crime, and even more painfully, the unthinkable outcome we have barely avoided. To me, it's just an exciting narrow escape, and despite her archery faux pas, we remain on good terms (Should that be faux coup?). I will continue to stay with them on odd occasions until my university years. I also retain the memory of that day in a small but distinct duelling scar on my right cheek.

Despite the distance they keep from the rest of my family, they are a jolly, welcoming lot, and seem to love having me. Although he's never there at the same time, Derrick is often mentioned, and his influence in the family is palpable. It's on one visit to their house at the age of maybe eight or nine, throwing stones at a row of garden canes, with no mature concept of range finding, that I put one straight through the rear window of a van parked in the driveway beyond.

It turns out to be Derrick's, parked there while he's working overseas. Even though I've never seen this mythical creature, my father, the thought of breaking his car window fills me with a dread over and beyond that of the casual miscreant. I'm devastated, and burst into tears of remorse and terror when the van's ownership is revealed. It takes days to convince me that the sky will not fall, and it's not until much later, at home again, when my mother conveys the message that my father has – although annoyed by the event – "decided not to take it any further," that I can begin to relax. Extraordinary, the force even an absent and practically anonymous figure can exert! The spectre of my distant father will continue to register its pull over the coming years, growing and fading like that of an infrequently visiting comet, until we finally meet. But more on that later.

The last member of my paternal strand is uncle Kenneth.

Kenneth is the glamour-boy of the family. Incredibly handsome, muscular, full of life, with a beautiful wife, Iona – who is exotically Scottish. He lives near Leicester, and whirls in and out of the family's life like a tornado. If I am there when he visits Joan or his parents, I am sure to be fêted royally. He always brings presents, plays cowboys and Indians with me and Valerie, and takes me for a ride on his Lambretta; not on the pillion – I am too little – but squeezed in front between him and the knee-guard, squinting into the wind over the handlebars like a dog out of a car window. I'm aware of the privilege, but terrified. When

History of a Daft A'porth

I'm older, I will stay once or twice with him and his family in Market Harborough, relishing their even more up-market, sophisticated way of life. (They live in a bungalow! They have a shower! They go abroad on holiday!)
He and Iona will divorce when I am sixteen, and I will be devastated, because they were the perfect couple, and perfect couples don't fall apart. Also, possibly because I have always had a secret crush on her.
All that is to come. My close family, and those who nurture and enclose me, are mummy, nannie, and grandad. I enjoy the occasional company of various male relatives in the semi-estranged branch, but there is no consistent male role-model for me. (Apart from grandad – but he doesn't count really!)

Then, one day,
"Peter, this is my friend Fred."
Out on a walk, my mother has arranged to meet this strange man, presumably deciding that the house wouldn't be a good place to begin the acquaintance.
"Hello."
"Hello."
Is there something prescient in the mind of even a five-year old child, that alerts them to a relationship that will not go well? Or is every child who is confronted with a rival for their single parent's affection struck with apprehension? Whatever the cause, I'm instantly wary of this man. He's obviously making an effort to be jolly, and to engage with me, but there's something about him that holds me back.
He's tall, slim but solid, balding, with a firm, forceful look.
It turns out that he and my mother are 'going out.'
This means she often disappears of an evening, heavily made-up, leaving me in the company of nannie, grandad, and the Big Book (latterly also, a children's *Treasure Island*, which I devour along with my bedtime cornflakes). It also means excursions, the three of us together, during which Fred talks to me about his family, some nature stuff, and other easy topics. Now and then we go away for a day to the seaside or a big park. Things progress. He

seems knowledgeable, calm, friendly – in his way. They see each other more often. He meets the parents – my grandmother and grandfather. He works, apparently, as some sort of jack-of-all-trades-come-handyman for various proprietors of industrial or landed bodies, and moves around from job to job as the work takes him. Mummy seems smitten. We visit his parents, and all his nearby relatives descend on their house for a family gathering. I am spoiled rotten by the various cousins, uncles and aunties.

It's also occasion for a minor epiphany.

I'm offered a piece of home-made apple pie.

What will endure as a source of impenetrable mystery to me, is that at some time before this moment I have convinced myself – I know not how – that I detest apple pie. I will not eat it.

A plate of it, with cream, is thrust under my nose.

"I don't like it!"

"You don't like apple pie?" Some relative of Fred's, "There must be sommat wrong with thee if tha dun't like apple pie!"

Stiff with propriety, my mother glares at me, and 'suggests' with barely restrained irritation, "Just try a bit, luv."

Recognising the constraints of politesse, and the veiled threat, I obey – my eyes scrunched up against the horror.

Oh my lord, what is this? Not at all what I expected! It's heavenly! This could be better than ice cream with a flake!

What on earth have I been doing for the whole of my short life, denying myself the ecstatic pleasure of this particular confection? Has someone once told me I didn't like apple pie? Even at this tender age my eyes are opened to what a disastrous effect blind prejudice can have. What a fool I've been! Opinions formed without evidence. Is this the beginning of my quest for rationality in the world? No truth without proof? Apple pie, and the search for scientific method?

I request a second helping.

The day comes when Fred, mummy, and I move away to set up home I know not yet where, leaving behind the familiar warm comfort of nannie and grandad's house. We travel in the back of a removal van as it takes what little furniture we have to our new home. It seems to take forever, but we finally arrive.

The Folly is a tiny one-up one-down whitewashed cottage perched halfway up a hill in Herefordshire overlooking the Black Mountains in Wales, and about half a mile from the Welsh border. There is a farm, also about half a mile away down a dirt track, where Fred currently works. Apart from that, no neighbours, just countryside, a pine plantation, and fields. The nearest town is Hay on Wye, twenty miles away. Closer, about two miles away, and just over the border, is the tiny hamlet of Evenjobb, where I am to attend school. I'm to go to school in Wales... whatever that is.

We arrive in early summer, and it's not as bad as I dreaded. We have a small garden in which we grow vegetables – including sweet corn, an absolute revelation for me – fresh corn on the cob! We go for long walks down the surrounding lanes, and I play out a lot by myself. I make friends with the neighbouring farmer and his family, a jolly lot. The children help me explore their farm and introduce me to the livestock. So I am often found there trying to convince one or other of their flock of sheep to be my pet. It never works, and I am finally discouraged from this pursuit when one day I find the semi-decayed corpse of one of them sprawled grotesquely at the base of a hedgerow. I'm brave enough to nudge it with my foot; the cadaver rolls down, and reveals itself to be full of fat wriggling maggots. This, along with the cockroach incident is a formative part of my introduction to the realities of nature's bounty.

The Folly is even more poorly appurtenanced than my grandparents' house. We have no electricity, no gas, and no running water. Set into the hillside, the house is more like a cave with doors and windows. There's a small open fire with a range (which we're used to, of course), fuelled by gathered wood, but all other heat and light comes from paraffin heaters and lamps. We buy a small primus stove to boil the kettle when the fire is not made. Each paraffin apparatus needs to be vigorously pumped up to pressurise the vapour before being lit, and similarly attended to at regular intervals as the pressure drops during use. We're going to develop muscles!

Water supply is even more primitive. It has to be brought regularly in a pail from a spring that surfaces alongside the approach track, about a hundred yards away from the house. This often turns out to be my job, and lugging a pail full of water that distance is a chore and a half for a small child. In winter, it's a nightmare. This is a time and a land of thick and bitter frosts, and it is a torment for me to trudge through the freezing air, break the sometimes thick and resistant plate of ice on the surface, plunge the bucket into the glacial water – inevitably soaking my hands – and totter unsteadily back to the house on the ice-glazed track. The pleasures of snowmen and snowball fights only partly compensate for the battle we have to wage with the penetrating cold that invades the house and our lives in winter.

We do have some light relief. These are the days long before we can even dream of a television, but we have a radio, which is on almost all and every evening. Its power comes from two accumulator (wet-cell) batteries, each the size of half a house brick, which have to be recharged every couple of weeks. To achieve this, my mother and I first carefully disconnect their terminals, then, keeping them scrupulously upright for the entire journey (like car batteries, they're full of acid), we walk to Evenjobb, take the bus to Hereford – the nearest place with an electrical appliances shop, which we walk to in the town centre, and exchange the exhausted batteries for freshly charged ones. We pay the recharging fee, and with equal regard to the corrosive contents, we make the return journey. A round trip of about fifty miles so we can listen to The Archers!

Getting almost anywhere involves a fair old trek of some kind; even school. For this, I walk the two miles there and back every day across several fields, over a tiny bridge or two that cross the stream feeding our spring, and finally along the road into the village.

The school is tiny – only one class of mixed aged children. I settle in without any issues, make friends right away, and feel

History of a Daft A'porth

accepted very quickly. This early lesson in adaptability will serve me well over the coming years.

Although very small, very rural, and Welsh, the school teaches in English, it being long before Welsh nationalism resurges to reclaim language, literature, and politics. There is, however, one event which dominates the school calendar, and demands some linguistic acrobatics from we anglophones.

The Eisteddfod.

For weeks, months even, leading up to this celebration of national culture and pride, we are steeped in the history, song, and poetry of Wales. Those deemed talented enough, (not me!) are given a solo piece to learn, and all of us set to, memorising *Land of our Fathers* in the Welsh language, which we will perform at the eisteddfod. It is hard: Welsh does not trip easily off our English-bred tongues. But we master it, and on the allotted day, pile onto the coach and set off for Aberdare, where the Eisteddfod is to take place. Once again, time will deprive me of most memories of the event itself. I will remember that we give a spirited rendition of our song, in a grand marquee, in front of a packed audience, and are rewarded with fulsome applause. The pride we feel afterwards will last a lifetime. Sadly, the words of the song will not be so easily retained, and my only remaining adult hold on Welsh will be my ability to pronounce the longest village name in Wales...

Llanfairpwllgwyngyllgogerychwyrndrobwllllantysiliogogogoch.

Not a great deal of use if you need to get somewhere else in Wales, but a minor triumph that I will in later life bring out of its bag at gatherings, when enough alcohol and/or jolly competitiveness encourages.

I'm aware that my relationship with Fred is not maturing into one you might call full of affection.

I'm beginning to think he actually dislikes me. When we're out for walks, or playing word-games as a family in the evenings, he dons the role of wise elder: naming wild flowers and trees; pointing out edible fruit in the hedgerows; explaining country lore; helping with vocabulary; which – give him his due – I find intrinsically interesting, but if I don't immediately conform to his wishes regarding behaviour, he is oppressively strict.

I read a lot, and am familiar with the different forms of parenting portrayed in books. There is the doting, indulgent kind, for whom even the wickedest child is a prince or princess; there is the wise, strict but fair and loving kind; there is the 'absent' parent who hardly notices the child at all, and there is the cruel kind – the step-mother of Cinderella nightmare, for whom the chores are never done, and with whom you may never go to the ball. I do not see anything of the first three in Fred, and increasingly feel myself living under an authoritarian thumb. Even my mother seems to be stricter these days. I spend as much time out of the house as possible, but whenever I am unavoidably in Fred's company, I am aware that his word is law. Any attempt on my part to disagree, to contradict, or disobey, is met with anger and menace. I am smacked frequently. Even in these times, when smacking children is acceptable, recommended even, I know that most of my so-called misdemeanours don't merit the level of rancour I receive. I'm also acutely aware – and this is worse – that what is far more important is the total lack of affection he shows me. I know what affection is. I've had lots of it from my mother and grandparents, and it's a powerful force. Children are as capable of forgiving unreasonable behaviour from parents as pet dogs are from their owners. If they believe they are loved, then, just like dogs, they will endure physical and psychological pain, and still love the offender. But between Fred and me there is absolutely nothing. A void. I see it in his eyes. I'm an impediment, an obstacle to a relatively easy life with my mother. Why should he have to drag this kid around, contribute to his education, feed and clothe him, and smile whilst doing it? I develop an instinct for avoiding him, but living in our cramped circumstances doesn't allow me complete escape, and I still suffer his spleen from time to time. There's never a moment of gentleness, rarely of praise, and that, only in front of my mother.

History of a Daft A'porth

Because of the itinerant nature of Fred's work, each post he takes lasts no more than a few months, a year at most, and at the end of every one, we have to move. He works as a farm labourer, estate worker, gamekeeper of sorts, and various other jobs, all over Herefordshire, Shropshire, and Gloucestershire. They all seem to have some kind of tied accommodation – some better than others, into which we decamp for the duration of his contract. After the Folly, we spend six months in a tiny caravan in a field adjacent to our next accommodation – Pheasant Cottage – until it becomes available. During this time, rather oddly for a caravan dweller, I have a pet tortoise. I suppose a dog in a small caravan would be a trial, and I have to make do with the meagre companionship of my reptilian sidekick. At some point it absents itself for a period of several weeks before mysteriously re-appearing. I assume it's the same one; I have no proof!

Living in a cramped and pokey caravan does nothing to improve our family dynamics, and it's only the mild summer weather that enables me to escape for sufficiently long periods when Fred is home. I can't wait for the space afforded by the comparatively palatial dwelling that awaits us.

We move into Pheasant Cottage for a period also of only about six months, but during which I luxuriate in the fact that it has its own orchard full of damsons and apples. There's such an abundance of fruit, that my mother goes slightly jam-crazy. The pantry at the back of the house ends up with so many jars in it, I wonder where, and from whom, she could possibly amass such a quantity. When we eventually move, a large number of them accompany us in various cardboard boxes, like protesting little rattling pets, to our next, and to subsequent, lodgings.

I have a whole summer holiday helping out on a nearby farm. The glorious weather allows me to spend day after day following a combine harvester with other child "helpers," pushing the hay bales it lays, like some gigantic field-crawling insect, to the sides of the fields, and watching rabbits run in terror as the last central stand of the waist-high grass in which they have retreated is cut down. Evenings are spent climbing around in the barns where the bales are stored, sliding down the slippery bundles, and playing castles in their irregular stacks. We're reprimanded by adults warning how dangerous it is: the stacks can move – collapse, even, and children can be trapped and suffocated. Of course, we pay no heed, and none of us suffers any harm worse than scraped knees.

A summer later, we have moved on again. We're now in Shropshire, around fifteen miles from Shrewsbury, and just outside Church Stretton, where I now go to school on the bus. Our accommodation of the day backs onto flatlands bordering the River Severn, and it floods – extensively. Contrarily, the weather following this is dry and hot, and I take full advantage of the bright skies to wade out, like Neptune striding the waves, into the reed-tufted expanse of shallow water filling the surrounding fields. The knee-deep water is clear and warm, and I am captivated by the teeming mass of small creatures that dart and spin everywhere. This shimmering playground lasts for weeks, its horizons gradually contracting under the persistent sun, until the river's original course is restored. Regularly out in it, far from the house, I pay no thought to the peril that can await a small child alone even in shallow water. Neither do my parents, apparently; all that seems to concern my mother is that I return in not too muddy a state.

These activities keep me away from the house for long periods. It means I'm out from under the severity of Fred's controlling hand and eye. Not unaware of the freedom and grace it gives me, I become more and more independent and adventurous in my outings. Even though still a child of only six or seven years, I'm happy to explore countryside, woods, streams, and lanes on my own, and have no sense of danger in doing so. Quite the contrary, in fact; I'm so conscious of my stepfather's continuingly belligerent attitude toward me, that being alone, roaming the wild and fascinating outdoors that surrounds our home (whichever one it may be at the time), endows me with a confidence and sense of myself that is suppressed only when I return home. Fred's need to dominate, and to ensure that any

History of a Daft A'porth

kind of dissent is stifled, is creating a growing trepidation in me when in his presence: fear of expressing myself, of any disagreement, of asking for something that he will decree outrageous or selfish, or of failing to obey an instruction in a sufficiently rapid and correct manner. His rules of behaviour are absurdly strict, and if not adhered to, elicit aggressive and intimidating responses. Not only am I regularly shouted at and slapped by him, but my mother is also encouraged to use these tactics. Sadly, despite what even I can detect is reluctance, she often goes along with this. I have more than one occasion to wait, terrified, as she climbs the stairs to my room, and as she emerges from the stairwell, I see from my bed that she is carrying the belt with which she will administer a series of blows to reprimand me for my "cheek," or other misdemeanours. They may not be as hard as she could make them, but they leave more than a physical mark, nonetheless.

This is to be my life for the foreseeable future, and pragmatically, I get used to it. I adapt. I modify my behaviour to accommodate these particular everyday challenges, and to mitigate the worst of Fred's ire. With a measure of success. My major strategy of being 'out' as much as possible is very effective, removing me from most zones of conflict. Mealtimes, evenings, and bedtime, however, remain a trial, and I have to bring many other tactics into play: reading, making models in my room, drawing; anything that keeps me under the radar.

We continue to move house regularly, following Fred's short-term jobs, inhabiting variously cottage, lodge, house, flat, whatever goes with the work. I decant to a new school whenever his change of job, and therefore our home, demands.

I shall attend, in all, eleven primary schools, and as an adult, will wonder how I attained *any* kind of education. But I did, and I shall remain forever grateful for it to my teachers (nearly all of whom, because of our rather brief acquaintance, I will forget), and to the genes I inherited that allowed me to benefit from their skills, patience, and expertise.

Peter Benson

I have three years of this dual existence – an uncomfortable mix of the idyllic settings of Laurie Lee's *Cider with Rosie,* and the emotional poverty of Dickens' young Pip in *Great Expectations* (my mother struggling to fill the Joe Gargery role). The result of this febrile situation, and the strategies I adopt to cope with it, is that I at least develop a strong sense of independence, of both thought and action. I learn to be content when alone, to confront and solve problems, to be adventurous and exploratory, and early on, to see the world of adults for what it is: complex, difficult, fascinating, and often roundly disappointing. I also develop a profound distaste for authority – arbitrary or otherwise – and a tendency to kick back at it which will stand me in good stead in later life.

It will also cause me more than a few problems!

History of a Daft A'porth

Chapter 4: Mr Taylor

Education is not the filling of a pot, but the lighting of a fire.
W.B. Yeats

I'm 9 now: old enough to begin an interest in the wider world, and to listen to the news on the radio. It's full of the Rome summer Olympics and Sputnik 5 returning safely to Earth with its cute little doggy crew of Belka and Strelka. In Hamburg, a newly formed music group has its first gig. It'll be a while yet before they have any real impact on my life, and the event goes almost completely unnoticed in Britain. Apparently, they decide to call themselves *The Beatles*. Odd choice...!

Fred's work takes him back to Halifax. During the previous year, my mother finally divorced Derrick, and she and Fred have married. This brings another significant change for me.
One's identity, even when very young, is closely tied to one's name. It defines us possibly even more as children, before our life experiences and developing personality begin to assume more weight on the scales of self-awareness. To my disgust, and despite my vigorous protest, our surname – my surname – becomes his: Horsfield.
The origin of this, my future, educated self will conclude, is possibly French ('Hors' – meaning outside, beyond), but to any of my so-called friends, it's unquestionably 'horse.' This leads inevitably to a host of more or less vulgar nicknames based on a theme. Horse-muck, horse-do, horse-poo, etc... etc... etc... These soubriquets will plague me through primary and secondary school until I am finally able to rid myself of them. Until that moment, they are yet another torment that Fred has managed to inflict on me, this time with his very name.
We move into a tiny one-up one-down terraced cottage: part of a cluster of houses in a small valley on the very outskirts of the town. An area known as Shibden Fold, about a mile from the

historic Shibden Hall, famous for its nineteenth century resident, the formidable Anne Lister. At least I'll see my gran more often now; she still lives on the north side of the town, and we visit frequently. My lovely grandad, who used to take down the 'big book' from its imaginary shelf to read me stories, passed quietly away last year, and I have been so distanced from that world, so caught up in my own universe of attempted escape; I have become so estranged from them, that the report of his death has hardly registered. It is only later that the sadness of this loss will affect me, and later still the guilt of not feeling it at the time.

My gran, Alice, does not like to come to ours. From the very start, she 'had a feeling' about Fred, and holds him in much the same contempt as I do. Would that my mother had listened to her...

So it's mostly my mum and me going to my gran's for Sunday tea, or, when I'm older, me going there after school to spend as much time away from Fred as I can. I pass many hours at my gran's even-smaller-than-our house. Later, it'll be more still.

The main road between Halifax and Bradford cuts through the countryside between Shibden Fold and a large park with a lake (Shibden Park). Fred works here for the council, renting out rowing boats to holidaymakers. Our house – number 12 Shibden Fold – is one of a handful of similar Victorian workers' cottages in the tiny hamlet. There are a couple of larger, better ones. One of these belongs to a German family who run a market garden in the fields next to their house, and with whose children – Peter, Annalie, and Erna – I become friends. Compared to ours, their house is a veritable palace. I know this because I've been inside – once. Not more than once, because the parents and the grandfather are, at the same time, extremely reserved, private, workaholics, and just a bit scary. Britain at this time is very 'pre-multi-cultural.' I have never met 'foreigners' before, and although their English is good, they have an air of the otherworldly, that for a naïve like me is slightly intimidating. Later, as a better-read adolescent, I will wonder whether some

History of a Daft A'porth

terrible wartime experience brought them to England, to this backwater of Halifax, and if it has made them wary of getting close to people. However, neither as a child, nor later, do I ask that question; the children are of my world, their parents and grandfather, of theirs.

Our house has a miniscule living room. Off it, is what is laughingly called a kitchenette: a space inside the street door with barely enough room for a gas stove and a sink. Up the stairs, which lead directly off the "kitchenette," is a single bedroom. To accommodate me, Fred partitions off a corner of this room and puts in a single bed. The space is so limited that the foot of this bed sticks out into the main bedroom inside a little box. My 'room' is not even the full length of a bed.

There's no hot water in the house, and no toilet. The nearest 'facilities' are situated a good 50 metres away at the end of the next block of houses. They consist of an open brick shed containing a wooden seat with a hole in it and a pan under. They abut a similar open shed, in which stand the dustbins for all of the community. It's to this block that I make my way, rain or shine, night or day, with no privacy apart from the fact that it closely faces the blank end of the adjacent row of houses.

My 'bedroom' is separated from that of my parents only by a curtain – through which I occasionally hear the muffled and repressed sounds of what I eventually realise must be sex. This, the trials of washing in the cramped space between cooker and sink, and those of the trip back and forth past overflowing bins to the stinking latrines, will remain forever the most enduringly embarrassing and humiliating aspects of my childhood. Sometimes, having suffered one or another of these demeaning, and depressing episodes, it all seems too much to bear; I am as despairing again as that four-year-old burying his head and his anxieties in the armchair.

During this period, my mother becomes the main breadwinner, working in a factory making brass fittings. She sometimes gets back just before my bedtime, her fingers glittering with brass filings, with grease smeared on her face. Often, on these occasions, she brings me home a little treat, my favourite being a bottle of Lucozade! Well before the time when sugar attains infamy as a devil's food, this tartrazine-infused fizz is a favourite tipple, and its appearance a highlight of my week.

Unlike my mother, Fred has a relatively easy job at the boating lake. Despite our testy relationship, he knows I'm practical, and in my non-school time, he allows me to help. He has an even easier time of it if I'm there, so it's motivated by self-interest rather than bonhomie. We develop an unspoken clandestine agreement over pocketing some of the fees that the punters pay to hire the boats. My first income! Albeit gained à la *Artful Dodger*, under the tutelage of my own *Fagin*. Over the course of the long school summer holidays I am often left completely in charge of the boats by my devious step-father, who skives off for a smoke or whatever he gets up to. I become an expert rower, adept at encouraging the punters, organising and physically manipulating the boats, and, as I am unpaid, raking off a small profit for myself – without depleting the takings sufficiently to arouse suspicion!

I struggle with the morality of this, and finally, my conscience getting the upper hand, I have to give it up.

Having got somewhat accustomed to an income stream, albeit paltry, I hunt around for a replacement, and, as luck would have it, something turns up out of the blue. Calling in regularly for sweets on my way to school, I have got to know my local newsagent quite well, and when he loses a paper boy to arcane teenage pursuits, he asks me to take over the round. It means getting up earlier, but I eagerly accept. It's tedious; unpleasant in bad weather, but apparently I do such a good job, he offers me an additional route... and then a further one in the evening. I somehow manage to do three paper rounds (including weekends), get to school on time, do all my chores, and still play out with all my mates. Compared to many of the kids I knock around with, I am the king of commerce! It's an early lesson for me in the freedom and independence that a steady income can bring, and in the rewards of hard work and application.

History of a Daft A'porth

But there's still school.

Salterlee Primary is my ultimate primary school. It sits high up on a hill about a mile away from our house, across a couple of fields, over a couple of walls, and 'up the road a bit.' As luck would have it, it is also at the far end of one of my paper rounds, so that's a bonus!

It's a tiny two-classrooms-and-a-hall-school, with two playgrounds: one for infants, and one for the 'big kids.' There are only around thirty to thirty-five pupils on the roll, and a small staff including the head-come-junior-teacher: Mr Taylor.

I have a few memories of teachers in previous schools who have given me a moment of insight or delight; how to draw arms with elbows rather than curved like horseshoes; learning to read; eisteddfod singing. But Allan Taylor is unlike any teacher I've known before, and is the first truly inspirational person I have ever encountered. He arrives as replacement for the retiring previous head when I have already been there for a few months, and brings with him the bright new spirit of child-centred teaching that began to flower in many schools in the late fifties and early sixties.

My University friend Andy Hargreaves, after a distinguished career as an educator and academic, will write in his affectionate and moving autobiography (aptly entitled just that... *Moving*), about the profound and long-lasting effect a dedicated and enlightened teacher can have on a child, and particularly on those children who seem to be in just the right place at just the right time. He mentions, and I am very happy to repeat it, Mary Hindle – his teacher when he was eleven, who inspired him to learn, to explore, and to achieve so much.

Reading Andy's book in my late sixties will finally – after years of prevarication – provide me with the final impetus to write my own, and it is Allan Taylor who inspires *me* so much as a child.

He calls us by our first names, not by our surnames; he does not use the ruler on our knuckles to punish us; he begins to teach us German! German! Not by rote grammar and vocabulary – but by fun question and answer. He teaches us the game of chess, and we read and listen to great stories by the likes of Dickens, Stephenson, and Defoe. Music becomes a daily part of our lives; listening to it, singing it, and rudimentary attempts at making it on various things that one hits, shakes, or scrapes. A record player is purchased, and we listen to its fantastical output. The Juniors (my class) are taken to Shibden Park to play cricket. We go on nature walks, bringing back arms and jars full of 'specimens,' animal, vegetable, and mineral, and we plant bulbs, which having sprouted, we proudly take home, (where, of course, they immediately die). We even do country dance, this though, is perhaps one step too far for me just now; I'll only fully discover the joys of English folk dance, with its sometimes wild, tribal music and frenetic energy, as a grown man of thirty.

After my grandad (whose long-ago influence it is difficult now for me to measure), Mr Taylor is the first substantial positive male role model of my life, and for that alone, as well as for everything else he embodies, I will owe him a greater debt than either of us are aware of at the time. He shows me that a man can wield authority with wisdom and gentleness, can encourage exploration of thought without wild condemnation of error, and can impart knowledge without the need for gratitude or cowed obeisance. He's the first adult male ever to engage me in a 'grown-up' conversation. Looking back, I'll recall always being treated by him, as a ten and eleven-year-old, with respect and a regard for my opinions. If one ever needs to look for heroes, one will find them aplenty amongst those teachers who imbue our children with a passion for learning, a respect for others, and a sense of human dignity.

Near the end of my last year at Salterlee I'm entered for the Eleven Plus, an exam for children in their final year at primary school that's the first in a series of similar steps that will forever divide those who are able – for one reason or another – to do well in *exactly this sort of exam*, from those who – for one reason or another – are not!

Along with some of my class mates, I'm assessed as having a combination of sufficient native wit, determination, and ability to absorb the *'right'* kind of knowledge, to be capable of passing this exam. Those who 'fail' this ridiculously segregating measure, will be consigned to what British society considers the lower ranks: the secondary modern school. Those who pass it will go to one of the grammar or technical high schools, to be bullied and sneered at as 'toffs,' for the next seven years by their erstwhile primary school classmates (those of us, that is, who don't leave at the minimum age of 15). The Eleven Plus is a precursor to the inflation of the exams and testing system that will plague English schools in later years, condemn many children to a less-than sympathetic education, make those less academically gifted and/or lucky, as 'lower ability,' and make many feel like failures?

Two of us pass...Time to move on again; on and 'up,' they tell me...

Peter Benson

Chapter 5:   Secondary School and other animals

Friendship is the hardest thing in the world to explain. It's not something you learn in school. But if you haven't learned the meaning of friendship, you really haven't learned anything.

Muhammad Ali

'Up' to big school. That's what parents call it... 'Big school!' And it is big! Halifax Technical High School. It aspires to be seen as on a par with the posher schools in the region. Indeed, shortly after I leave, in 1969, it will achieve the status of grammar school.

As far as I know, there is no connection between those two events!

Compared to the intimate little two-classroom primary I left a long summer holiday ago, I've landed on another planet. We visited the school shortly after my eleven plus, my mother and I, but it didn't really sink in then. It was a foul day, and the area was shrouded in thick mist, reducing the visible dimensions of the school to manageable proportions.

When I arrive for my actual first day, however, it's clear and bright, and I step into an aircraft carrier of a school. I'm wearing – alongside the other lambs bleating their way into the assembly hall – shiny new blazer, shiny new grey short pants, a new school cap *(WHICH MUST BE WORN AT ALL TIMES WHEN TRAVELLING TO OR FROM SCHOOL!)* and clutching my shiny new satchel (real leather!)

The school is situated on the north edge of the town, and to get there, in contrast to my earlier bucolic stroll through farmland and back lanes, I have to catch the bus: two, in fact. The first, after a ten-minute walk to the busy main road, takes me into town, where I join the heaving masses of children gathered at the designated school bus stops. Kids from all the out-of-town schools gather here, including those from the secondary modern, and, I discover, those from Heath Grammar... our arch rivals. They are the ones that school honour dictates we should try to beat at cricket, rugby, and football, and they are the ones,

History of a Daft A'porth

paradoxically, that *we* regard as 'toffs.' We have one rugby side, they have three, and we usually play their lower fifteen. Six years hence it will be a source of immense pride, when I am stand-off-half in the side that beats their first fifteen for the very first time, then goes on to also beat them in the seven-a-side regional tournament. But that's a world away...

The second bus is a zoo. The kids in it range from the innocents – mostly the lower years, and especially the 'fags' (first -years) – to the positively feral veterans. It is on these buses that I witness the most cruel bullying. This happens right from the very first day. Luckily for me, I am not one of those picked on. In the playground or street, you can generally run away; on the bus, there is no escape, you're trapped. 'Weaker' children are regularly slapped, punched, extorted, and reduced to sobs by the ruling 'elite.' I have seen bullying and dominance at primary school, but this landscape of wolves chewing up puppies is new to me. I am not particularly brave, but fortunately I appear to fit into the 'leave 'em alone' category, as I *do* get mostly left alone – thank goodness. There is one occasion that stands out, however. In my third year, when one of the older bullies has been pushing around a close friend of mine, Stuart. Heart in mouth, I confront him. I tell him to stop. He doesn't take kindly to this, and grabs me by the lapels, upon which, to my own surprise, I land the first of the only two uppercuts of my life on his jaw, jerking him backwards several inches. Tears come to his eyes, and he backs off, then silently walks away. Astonishingly, I win the day. He never touches either of us again. Stuart is awe-struck and fulsomely grateful. I am quite simply stunned by what I've done, and left wondering where the courage to do it came from! I don't know it yet, but I will have occasion to draw on it again.

School life slips into a routine. It's both different from primary school, and also remarkably similar. Lessons are separated more rigidly, and taught by subject-teachers, but we arrive, play football (some better than others!), line up, go in, have assembly, morning lessons, lunch, afternoon lessons, and then go home. Same old same old. We exist in the school bubble. We're almost totally unaware of the world outside. Unaware that, in October of that year -1962 – while we face up to bullies in bus and playground to see who will back down first, much the same kind of confrontation is being played out far away over the sea by two unimaginably powerful men also tussling for position. Except, the outcome hanging on this confrontation is not merely a bloody nose, but the very end of the world. The Cuban Missile Crisis hits the news worldwide, and the world holds its breath. The two men come to an arrangement; the world breathes again, and Halifax Technical High School is not incinerated – much to the possible regret of some.

My twelfth birthday arrives. At home, there's been a gradual deterioration in relations with Fred – already strained by my approaching teenage. I seem to get under his skin more and more each day. It's possible there are other reasons for his decreased level of tolerance, but if there are, I'm unaware of them. I just know that he can go off like a powder keg at the slightest thing. I'm becoming quite frightened. I haven't been actually scared of him for a while, just wary, and strategically sycophantic, but now it feels somehow more dangerous.

And so it proves to be. There are two incidents over the coming year that frighten the life out of me. On each occasion, I have somehow provoked his rage. Perhaps the trauma supresses my memory, but later I will never be able to fully recall what I have done. The result on the first occasion, whatever the cause, is rather than the usual slap round the head or on the legs, I'm grabbed and bundled up against him, and in his fury, within the grasp, he brings up his knee into my ribs. It's excruciatingly painful. I somehow wriggle free and flee the house, only returning much later when my mother comes home, and I cautiously ascertain that he has calmed down. I don't tell my mother what's happened: why, I'll never know. Maybe I have some kind of victim guilt; that it was somehow my fault... who knows?

Even when subsequent pain causes a visit to the doctor that reveals a cracked rib, I maintain it was from rough play out with

History of a Daft A'porth

my pals. I should have said something there and then; it might have avoided the next occurrence.

The origin of the conflict is a little clearer this time, I've denied being the cause of some problem that is patently not my responsibility. Things become heated. I should know better, but I feel I'm in the right here. We're in the tiny living-room of our house once more. Fred is cutting some vegetables with the carving knife on the table by the window. It develops into a shouting match, and suddenly, with a look of rage on his face he comes for me. I'm on the other side of the little room's settee, and he's advancing on me with a carving knife in his hand for God's sake! It may absolutely be that he forgets it's there; we can work out the odds on that. But I'm twelve! It's not uppermost in my mind that he's been a bit absent-minded here! I'm off round the settee heading for the door. Moving faster that I thought possible, I rocket into the street. I leg it like an Olympian down the track that serves our hamlet from the main road. I don't slow down. A few yards on, in full flight, I glance back. He's not following! I keep going till I'm far enough away in case he leaves the house. There's a telephone box just on the corner. I make it in there, keeping a terrified eye on the distant door. I'm shaking like a leaf in a gale, but manage to dial 999.

"Police, please!" I gasp into the mouthpiece.

Put through, half sobbing, I explain to the police officer on the other end, that my stepfather has just chased me around the settee with a carving knife. Calmly, he asks where I am, and gives me some instructions about keeping well clear; not that I need the advice! He assures me someone is on the way. An agonisingly long-seeming interval later, a tiny Panda car pulls up alongside me, and the driver, a sergeant so large and solid it seems impossible he fits in the car, gets out. Speaking softly, he gets me to retell the story, and advising me to "Wait there, son," goes up to the house, knocks, and is let in. He's in there for a good long time. I'm sat apprehensively on the ground by the phone box when he comes out. He crouches down by me, and says, "I don't want you to be frightened, son. I've had a word. You can go back in if you want; nothing's going to happen to you. He knows he shouldn't have done it, and he knows I'll be keeping an eye out. You'll be alright." Considering what has transpired, it would not be unreasonable of me to question his assessment of the situation. But something in the manner of this big, strong, friendly copper, his quiet confidence and the sense of the weight of his authority fills me with an unexpected sense of relief. Against exceptional odds, I believe him.

"Any more trouble, you just give me a ring" – he hands me a slip of paper with the station number on it. Then he gets back in his implausibly little car, waves, and drives off. I am left so enveloped by his personality and solidity that I grit my teeth, and go back in. And he's right. Incredibly, nothing happens! Fred just ignores me.

It's still not great from then on, but there is never again an incident as drastic or terrifying. I would give anything to have been party to the conversation that went on in our sitting room between that sergeant and my tyrant of a stepfather, but I will never find out. I will remain, nonetheless, deeply indebted to that wonderful, gentle, sturdy policeman, who that evening, I am happy to believe, saved my life.

The following day, the news of president John F Kennedy's assassination spreads out over the news networks. I may be only twelve years old, but it is such a widely and deeply felt catastrophe, that even I am touched by it; perhaps because I'm still in a high emotional state after my own escape from what could also be called – with some dramatic colouring – an assassination. It is probably my first real understanding of a significant political event, and certainly my first of a tragedy of such significance. The attack not just on Kennedy, but on the sense of optimism itself that his presidency has generated globally, affects me. Flawed though he is later revealed to be, Kennedy appeared to me a kind and liberal man. Perhaps I saw in him, and men like him, something that was missing from my own life, and the loss of such a figure, distant though he is, moves me in an unexpectedly profound way. As a child, I also find it disturbing that one so powerful and so protected can be

History of a Daft A'porth

obliterated so easily. Perhaps it spotlights for me the precarious nature of my own poorly defended situation.

There is an inevitable result of the subdued nocturnal murmurings I have had to suffer since we moved into Shibden Fold. My half-brother, Ian, is born. The house is already too small for two adults and *one* child, but Ian's cot is crammed into the space between the window and my mother's side of the bed.

At 12 years old, I don't take kindly to the new arrival. Had I experienced a different kind of childhood so far, would I feel differently? It's impossible to know. As it is, all I do feel is resentment. This is compounded by the fact that Fred obviously dotes on Ian. Although sticking to the traditional masculine roll of leaving all the domestic chores, including those concerning the baby, to my mother, he exhibits an obvious affection for Ian that's not lost on me, and as the baby grows, I begin to act towards him in a way that will leave me with a lingering source of shame later in life. I'm still made to go to bed well before my parents. Ian's frequently in his cot at the same time, and I find it beyond my power to resist waking him; provoking his tears by calling him and not letting him sleep. I do this repeatedly. There is so much pent-up rage within me, and as yet I am too immature to recognise it. I need a 'safe' target to vent it. So I am *not* kind to my baby brother. I use every opportunity when we are alone to tease and verbally torment him. Thankfully, I never resort to physical hurt, but nonetheless chafe and irritate him with a view to making him as much of a nuisance to Fred and my mother as possible. It is shameful behaviour, and even though its roots are indisputably in my shabby treatment at the hands of someone who should shelter and protect me, I will never truly forgive myself for it.

As Ian grows, and learns to talk, it becomes increasingly risky to subject him to teasing and provocation. Pragmatically, I ease off. Pricked by conscience, I try to become more of a big brother for him, taking him out to play, doing jigsaw puzzles, etc. Our relationship remains uneasy, however, and we will never become close. There will always remain a gap between us. He is Fred's son, and I am most definitely not. The anger inside me will remain bottled up for many years, occasionally redirected at my mother and at my gran. It also continues to be my default approach to any authority figure who has not thoroughly earned my respect. But at least I now stop deflecting it onto another innocent child.

Back in my school life, there are new experiences. Homework, for example. We didn't have that at primary school. No-one likes it! For me it takes up time I would otherwise spend outside with my friends. Also, my bedroom being so small, it means I have to endure even more time in the same room as Fred. It's a double blow.

Then there's organised sport. Sport at primary school was like an extension of the playground: loosely organised, inclusive, and slightly mad. Sport at secondary school is less forgiving, and can be brutally awful. It is either, on the one hand, activities we all like because they're easy, and we can all play; or on the other, activities a significant number of us hate, because we are – frankly – rubbish at them. Amongst the activities I'm rubbish at are football, rugby, and swimming. Particularly swimming. I firmly believe that my continued inability to swim as an adult – indeed my terror of being under water – will be due to our swimming teacher at school. Rather than learning to swim, I develop a pathological fear of being in the water, and, along with several other inadequates, spend swimming lessons either out of the pool on some spurious excuse or forged parental note, or else walking along the shallow end with our heads poking out like ducks in a row, pretending to 'swim.' I will find out sixty years later, that my university friend Andy Hargreaves, whose memoir inspired this one, has suffered the same swimming lesson anguish for the same reasons at the same time, although he does later learn to swim. It will be with huge relief, and great joy, that I will eventually watch my own children – properly and sympathetically coached – emerge from their initial hesitancy in the pool to become veritable mermaids, leaping and diving into the water, and flashing though it like dolphins leading a ship. I,

History of a Daft A'porth

however, will remain forever standing on the edge, getting occasionally splashed.

Those who are good at the various sports eventually represent the school, and dominate playground games, whilst the rest of us suffer the regular humiliation of being picked last – or nearly last– by the golden boys crowned as team captains during games lessons or breaktime matches.

I am not a bad runner, though. By my third year, I'm doing quite well in sports-day track events, and although I'm not on any school teams, I enjoy the show of support from other participants that accompanies even a second or third place. Events of strength, on the other hand, are not my forte. I realise I'm destined to be skinny. Even a sallie into the Charles Atlas Body-Building Course – a series of postal lessons in physique improvement – ends in nothing more than a lot of perspiration and wasted pocket money.

My previous school-hopping experience allows me to quickly make friends. I don't think there are any kids who have none, although there are those who stand out a little: what we at this age call 'weird,' When we later acquire more education and sensitivity, we will understand these targets of mockery to be shy, introverted, unsure of their sexuality, or victims of poor domestic circumstances that leave them depressed or cowed. My close friends and I fortunately have a nascent awareness of this, albeit in a very rudimentary way, and inflict only the peer-required minimum of scorn upon these less 'conventional' people. Despite the bullying, the mockery, and the marginalisation that is inevitable in any school – and ours is no exception, from what we hear beyond the gates – it appears we are relatively lucky. It all seems at a level that, although undeniably cruel, thankfully avoids tragedy.

My closest mates are the two Richards, Forrest and Heap. We have similar characters. We're all a bit bookish, we all do reasonably well in class, and we're all rubbish at organised sport. We're not amongst the hard kids, we don't smoke, and we quite like some of the lessons. It's a natural progression that we start to hang out together, and after a while we become, as they say, inseparable. Richard Forrest has an older brother, Robert, who's on the rugby team, and becomes head boy, but I think Richard's a bit intimidated by him. He seems to prefer our company to that of his big brother's. We're a sort of gang of three. If there's a project to do that needs volunteers – building a papier maché escarpment for geography open day, for example, or setting up some physics apparatus before the lesson – we're your lads, and eventually earn the surprisingly inoffensive nickname 'The Three Musketeers.' We start getting together outside school as well, and in the fifth form, even organise a party.

This is to take place at Richard Heap's house, and rather trendily, we believe, in the cellar. We deck it out with some home-made bunting, get in a keg of beer, (wow!) and lay on a bite to eat and some music. No-one comes. We've confirmed what we secretly suspected all along; as well as all the other things we are not, we are also not amongst the cool kids. The cool kids smoke in the bogs (toilets), talk about their – undoubtedly fictitious – sexual adventures, and dodge lessons. We, it has to be admitted, are swats. Nobody goes to a party thrown by swats, not even, it seems, other swats. Never mind. Now we have a whole keg of beer to ourselves, and end up not too unhappily inebriated by the end of the evening.

What really draws us together is the undeniable fact that we are geeks. Of a kind, anyway. Since I was old enough to be capable of doing them, I've loved construction kits. Particularly Airfix. These plastic cornucopias fascinate me. From the intricate shapes attached like tiny plastic fruit to their spikey plastic vines, it's possible to build the whole world. Airfix lays at your feet: aircraft, of course (a range from WWII), allies and enemies; cars, ships (from galleons to destroyers), figures (roman soldier, beefeater, Henry VIII), and military vehicles (tanks, armoured cars, field guns, etc). In the same way that the bitter-sweet-smelling polystyrene cement oozing from its metal tube magically and instantly binds together these three-dimensional puzzles, it is war that glues us together. Tanks, artillery, and

History of a Daft A'porth

other war machines. Both Richards, I discover, are equally fanatical collectors.

Airfix is so popular it even publishes a magazine for model enthusiasts (geeks). And that's what we are. In the magazine (monthly), there are articles on modifications that – with some polystyrene sheets, plasticine, balsa wood, a modelling knife or two, and plenty of modeller's paints – allow one to convert the off-the-shelf models into variants and later versions. It takes time and a steady hand, but I love it, and I'm proud of the results. Done properly, the conversions can look as if they were original kits. All three of us become proficient at this, and it turns into an obsession. We undertake war-games (at their houses – for obvious reasons I never entertain at mine), spending weeks attempting to write a comprehensive set of rules. This doesn't work out too well, leading to chaotic non-resolutions of our games, but it doesn't matter, we enjoy the thrill of battle anyway! Each of us ends up with a veritable army of units, most of which have been modified one way or another to a Mark 1 or a Mark 2, or even a completely different vehicle, and we pass endless evenings and weekends campaigning on the European and African fronts. Yes, we really are total geeks.

As school wears on, we three make the kind of progress one would expect. We don't get into trouble with the staff, we're never called to the head's sanctum. We take on small offices, such as putting out the hymn books before assembly and collecting them afterwards. We help backstage with the school plays, become classroom monitors and the like, and hang around out of school together all the time. We congregate with the other rejects on the edge of ball games that require more skill than we possess, and invent ones that don't. We're so close, we eventually decide to undertake a mutual financial escapade...

At around the age of fifteen, impelled by teenage bravado, we convince an older schoolmate with contacts to facilitate the purchase of a car. Our car! We've saved enough between us from hoarded pocket money, paper-rounds, and other spare-time jobs, to pay for a second-hand Ford Cortina from a dealer. The idea is that the three of us will jointly own this vehicle, and it'll be kept off-road in a friend's farm where it can be driven on a private track as a means for us to learn to drive. Eventually, we shall take jolly trips in it, and undoubtedly pick up girls. All subsequent motor-related expenses are to be shared between us. Oh, what fools these mortals be! That dealer will doubtless go on to teach the future Arthur Daley all he knows. The car turns out to be the kind of vehicle an old banger would regard with deep contempt. It's a total dog. 'Guaranteed' for three months, it keeps its word practically to the day. First, the electrics start to play up – indicators not working, no horn, and the like. Then the clutch begins to slip, and finally the steering develops a mind of its own; thank god we're on waste ground! Having ended bonnet down in the bushes, we traipse round to appeal to the dealer's better nature. He turns out not to have one. There is no refund. The car, following examination by another schoolmate's dad who knows about these things, is pronounced DOA. Would we had turned to him for advice beforehand! We receive a paltry sum for it as scrap value, and slink away to lick our wounds and curse our naivete. Daft a'porths, all three.

This mutual calamity is probably the beginning of the end. Like continental drift in reverse, the union between the Three Musketeers will begin to dissolve, and other interests will inexorably pull us apart.

In reality, they've probably already started to. At the age of thirteen, I joined the Air Cadets, having been toying with the idea of an eventual career in the RAF. I hadn't yet critically examined what being in the forces entails – dropping bombs, shooting and killing people, laying waste etc. I was just fascinated by aeroplanes. I loved to draw them – Spitfires, Hurricanes, Lancasters etc, and the idea of flying was increasingly in my mind. I was persuaded to join by a recently made friend from Crossley and Porter School. Ash was already a cadet, and it would be great fun, he insisted.

It's great fun. The uniform (provided) is a bit heavy and scratchy, but really smart. We do drill, learn about engines, aircraft recognition, navigation, and RAF life. There are several opportunities a year for flights in real service aircraft – even

History of a Daft A'porth

jets! We also go rifle shooting once a month. Now this, I'm good at. We use .22 rifles; they don't give you the kick that a full service .303 would, and are a lot easier to use. I discover I can shoot like Davy Crockett. I quickly earn my marksman's badge, (5 shots in the perimeter of an old penny at 25 yards), and then my sharpshooter's badge (The same at 50 yards). I go on to represent the squad in competition. Unused to this kind of success, when my running abilities also come into play, I am even more surprised...

The Air Cadets have large sports tournaments, and miraculously, I make it through the local competitions onto the Yorkshire region's team for the national cross-country event held in London, and I am awarded a travel allowance by the RAF. Fifteen years old, I am oblivious to the risks and to the horror spilling over from child-murderers Ian Brady and Myra Hindley across the Pennines: I pocket the cash, don my uniform, and hitch hike the two hundred miles south. Said uniform makes it a doddle.

Accommodation is in Nissen huts on an RAF base near Luton, and there are loads of us. I have a great time. We eat in the RAF mess, and mix with the servicemen and women of the base. I even win a few quid playing cards with some of the other boys in the billet on the evening before the competition. I'm full of myself!

The following day, the cross-country course knocks that out of me completely: ten punishing miles across Hampstead Heath in February. There are about two hundred participants, and I stagger home, completely wrecked, but an honourable 25th. The big surprise, however, is that after all the runners' positions are confirmed, our region wins. My team wins the event! There is a medal as big as a manhole cover for each of us, a certificate, and head-swelling pride. When I get back to my squadron (once more by dint of my thumb and my cadet uniform, braving hordes of mass murderers on route), I am a hero! *And* several quid better-off!

For some boys, (and girls, in the Venture Corps) this is the beginning of a career. Alas, despite my sporting success, my time in the squadron will be limited. The instructors are RAF officers or reserves, but the non-commissioned officers are all drawn from the cadets, and comprise: lance-corporal, corporal, sergeant, flight-sergeant, and warrant officer. If you behave, show willing, ability, authority, and promise, you can rise through these ranks, and eventually join the service as an officer cadet. My friend Ash makes it to corporal. We also have a sergeant, and a warrant officer who would frighten Windsor Davis. Under him we are rigorously drilled in our little hut and parade ground; sternly supervised at lessons and on the shooting range; vociferously knocked into shape as recognisable members of a cadet unit. We even come second in the national drill and formation marching competition.

We're a crack squad!

I, however, have an attitude, apparently. This is one of many manifestations of the lippy disposition which will from time to time bite me in the bottom. I've been expecting promotion. I've done well in all my tests; navigation, aircraft identification, service ranks, Morse code, basic RAF regulations, etc, and I'd thought it was inevitable I would get corporal. Not so, says the warrant officer; according to him, the officers find me a bit too clever for my own good. I talk back too much in lectures, and resist certain aspects of discipline. I'm not to receive my stripes. It's a blow, but worse is to come. My first experience of flight is as a passenger in a Chipmunk, the standard single-engine tandem-seater RAF training aircraft. The pilots know that we are flight-virgins, and avoid throwing us around wildly, but a Chipmunk is small and highly manoeuvrable; even the gentlest of turns feels giddy, and I become nauseous and scared. It's an echo of the nasty tummy I get on rollercoasters or high-rising swings, and will later feel as a pillion passenger on a speeding and steeply banking motorbike. I want the ground back. This is not good, flying appears to be not for me. It will be with a great deal of trepidation some seventeen or so years later, that I prepare to take my first commercial passenger flight, clenched up with the memory of this day. To my surprise and relief, the sensation will be totally different, and will not upset me at all.

History of a Daft A'porth

Here and now, though, once back on terra firma, the Air Cadets can only be downhill for me. Eventually, after two years as a recruit, I quit the squad.

I keep up with Ash, though, and once again, because he's always two steps ahead of me in the dizzy race through adolescence, I discover a whole new social life just when I begin to need one: the coffee bar.

There's a place in Halifax town centre where Ash and his mates regularly go. They're all mods: parkas, Gibson trousers, Beatles haircuts (Remember that group in Hamburg? They seem to be making some noise over here now); some even have a scooter. The coffee bar has blacklight, and thanks to the brightening chemicals in our white shirts and our toothpaste, we all glow like radioactive aliens. An unfortunate side effect for some is that the UV also makes your dandruff glow, a fact the more cruel gleefully and loudly point out – to the afflicted and everyone else. There's a juke-box, people dance occasionally; we drink coffee – no booze as yet – and some smoke. It's bohemian! We talk and talk, and act silly. We are pretty young things. I don't invite either of the Richards; I don't think they'll fit. I can be a dick, sometimes.

We're now in the fifth year, and I'm indisputably drifting away from my old friends. Airfix kits are far less attractive than in my earlier years. Also, rather astounding myself, I've somehow become quite good at football and cricket, and I'm playing regularly at breaktimes whenever there's a game. Because of this, my new team-mates now count me amongst their friends, and I am spending more time with them. I begin to edge away from geekdom, and rather callously, to abandon the loyalties of my former pals. We sporty lads are now also big enough and bold enough to get away with going to the pub, and I'm spending more than a few evenings a week with these new mates, becoming familiar with Halifax's licenced hostelries. All of a sudden, I feel a bit more grown-up. And sixth form is looming. School asks, am I staying on?

It depends...

Chapter 6: Sweet Sixteen

> Growing up is such a barbarous business, full of inconvenience and pimples.
>
> *J.M. Barrie*

1967: I'm Sixteen...
This year, the UK will apply for membership to the EEC; there will be the Summer of Love; Israel will decisively win the six-day war against the Arab nations. A lot will also happen to me.

In my sixteenth year, I will leave home; I will punch my stepfather; I will win school sporting colours; I will have my first girlfriend; I will change my name. And I will meet my father.
Yes, I'm staying on. I *shall* be coming back for the sixth form. It's not compulsory, many of my classmates are leaving to start work, but I want to continue my education.
Sixth form; with the prospect of eventually going to university. I'm lucky to be here, and I owe this to my mother.
Fred had categorically refused to support me in school any further, she tells me, but she has dug her heels in on this point, and insisted I be given the opportunity. I'm lucky enough to have done well at school, always coming somewhere in the first three or four in all subjects. I have won the occasional book prize for academic achievement: volumes I proudly chose from the local branch of WH Smiths. My mother can see that it would be a waste of potential and a cruel deprivation to pull me from school now, and has taken a rare stand against Fred.

Since she took up with him, my mother, Emily, has been an enigma to me. In the years before that watershed in my life, she was easy to understand: cuddly mummy, away at work in the day, but there for evenings and weekends to make buttered toast, play word games, and have tickling matches. She was kind, pretty, funny, and I adored her. Once shackled, however – as I began to see it – to this man who made my life miserable, bit by bit she slid from her pedestal. One's perception of one's parents

History of a Daft A'porth

changes irrevocably as one gets older, their human imperfections manifesting in subtle and not-so-subtle ways. You discover they make mistakes, they forget things, they tell lies, and they let you down. In the course of most childhoods, in stable, reasonable families, these cracks in the façade of perfect parenthood do not result in the whole edifice tumbling down; hopefully, our growing awareness of our own imperfections and idiosyncrasies inform and temper the irritation and disappointment we feel when confronted with fallibility in our parents. People we have actively chosen as friends are capable of such frailties, and we continue nonetheless to love them; don't our parents deserve the same clemency and forgiveness? We should see these 'faults' as simply a part of the person we admire and love, and we forgive them, as we hope ourselves to be forgiven.

The lens through which I view my mother's failings, however, is increasingly distorted; clouded by a growing sense of betrayal. A conviction that this person – my protector – could make it all better if she tried. But she doesn't. She is, in many respects, a strong woman. I have seen her stand up to people in argument or confrontation, and she's not one to keep her opinion to herself. She's quick to laugh, easy to talk to, and a spade, in my mother's lexicon, is very definitely something you dig with. Both practical and incredibly stubborn, she'll persist in a task until it's done. She is of course of a generation where women do all the domestic stuff, and although she's not the tidiest or most hygiene-conscious of cooks, I am well fed. She even encourages a love of fresh fruit and veg that anticipates the twenty-first century phenomenon of the gut biome. Strict and proper in company, she knows right from wrong, and is assiduous in passing this on to me. From her, I'm sure, I develop my strong (some may say overdeveloped!) sense of justice and fair-play. Incredibly hard working, and often exhausted on returning from her job, she nonetheless invested a great deal of her spare time in encouraging my early reading, writing, and exploration of the world, sharing in this way her love of books. I can see she's popular with friends and those work colleagues I may meet; some of whom I later discover, flirt with her outrageously. My mother has a buxom prettiness, and despite having all her teeth extracted, and a false set fitted, at the age of twenty-one (as a birthday present – corrective dentistry being beyond their means), she has a dazzling smile. Wearing make-up, jewellery, and her best dress, she has a glamorous, film-star quality about her. When we're alone together, she is affectionate and fun. There's much about her I admire. As the years pass in our new family unit, however, I'm increasingly convinced that she is in some way complicit with the almost daily persecution I have to endure. So: strong in many ways, but illogically weak in this. I cannot understand how she allows the situation to persist. It's obvious that she's aware of the fault lines between me and Fred, so why doesn't she just take me and leave? According to everything I've read, mothers are supposed protect their children, whatever the cost to themselves, and yet she does not conform to this universal law. Bizarrely, and confusingly, she will sometimes defend me to the point of having a plate of food thrown at her, yet on another occasion, she will comply with, even participate in, my thrashing on the legs with a slipper or belt. It's no wonder my feelings for her are in flux. Inevitably, by the time I reach my teens, my childhood loyalty to her is sufficiently battered, that the par-for-the-course adolescent contempt I exhibit is amplified by resentment. Sadly; inevitably; I lose my respect for, and closeness to her. Moving away permanently over the following decades, I will allow the geographical distance between us to become a void.

This void is further widened as I climb the educational staircase, and is deepened by the perceived superiority that my youthful arrogance tells me I consequently possess. We do see each other over the coming years, she visiting me, mostly, rather than me her, but the occasions are rare, and brief. Thirty-odd years hence, after the birth of my daughters, we will re-establish more regular and amicable contact, but I'll never again be capable of close affection for her, forever believing she sacrificed my childhood happiness to stay with Fred.

History of a Daft A'porth

Because of this, when she passes away in 2105, I will, as so often with my close family, be haunted by a leaden sense of guilt at the paucity of grief I feel for her.

But in 1967, my going to sixth form is one of those rare moments when she makes a stand, and I'm old enough and shrewd enough to be truly, truly grateful. Despite my gnawing resentment of her attachment to and love for Fred in the face of his treatment of me, I grudgingly recognise the strength and resistance she has mustered on this occasion for my benefit.

It's a whole new world in the lower sixth. We're now all prefects, a power which goes to the head of some, who have to be reminded of their privilege and responsibility. *Noblesse oblige!* Though we still wear uniform, suddenly we are treated as young adults. Teachers who, years ago, viciously whacked miscreants in my class for their misdemeanours, now call us by our first names, and – wonder of wonders – some even allow us to reciprocate with theirs! We have a common room, where we make tea and coffee, and there's a record player! Because we take only three or four subjects, we have free periods, during which we're supposed to study, of course, but which we typically use to lounge around in said common room, talking, drinking coffee, listening to records, and playing the aesthetes we feyly believe ourselves to be.

At some point close to the end of my previous year, I had been approached by Mr Bannister, the games master, who asked if I intended to stay on into sixth form. When I said yes, he wondered if I would consider joining the school rugby team. I nearly fell on the floor. Me?

It transpired he'd been made aware of my performance in the playground. Over my fifth year the break-time games of football had largely given way to touch-rugby, played usually with a rolled-up school cap (no longer required wearing after one's third year!). It seems I'd developed a talent for the game, was agile, and adept at avoiding the touch-tackles of my opponents: arching, dancing, and feinting my way around their outstretched fingers to score. This had been noted by those already in the school team, and passed on 'up the line.' Having ascended to sixth form, I'm more than delighted to accept his invitation, and thus embark on a sporting career in the school that will give me enormous pleasure, pride, and success. It culminates in the award of colours for representing the school on numerous occasions, including leading the seven-a-side rugby team to some small glories in national tournaments.

Our rugby coach, Howard Wroot, is also the physics teacher. Unlike his ultra-disciplined approach to the team, his physics teaching is madly idiosyncratic: magnetometers turn into wailing rock guitars, and oscilloscopes make weird howling noises. Frank, the tame polecat from the adjoining biology lab makes riotously disruptive incursions into our physics area. It's not uncommon for him to nibble the hairs on one's shins at a critical point during an experiment, or walk sparkily all over your electrical circuit. Table tennis balls bounce around the room in wild demonstrations of the coefficient of restitution, and home-made catapults measure elasticity by firing missiles out of the windows – with little thought for who may be passing. Over all this, Mr Wroot presides with manic enthusiasm. For me, in these crazy lessons and the intense atmosphere of the rugby team, he fills the gap left by Alan Taylor when I moved on from Salterlee – another male role model with whom we share humour, respect, and camaraderie, and who by doing so, encourages loyalty, affection, and dedication.

I train incredibly hard for the rugby team, and Howard confers on me the soubriquet of fittest boy in the school. Thanks to this graft, and some achievements on the field, I experience for the first time, not only the esprit-de-corps of vigorously competitive team sport (cross country doesn't do that for you), but also the heady sense of adulation from the whole school as you hold aloft a hard-won trophy in assembly.

I begin to sense I'm leaving my childhood behind. My boyhood pursuits no longer interest me; I've an eye to university. Trips to the pub with my mates – particularly the rugby team – though still illegal, become commonplace. We even sink the occasional pint or two with our teachers... imagine! However, I've not yet achieved the pinnacle of that adolescent transition into manhood. I do not have a girlfriend.

Several of my mates are going out with girls from one school or another (bragging constantly about how 'far' they've gone), but I haven't yet had the courage or opportunity to emulate them.

Living at home doesn't help. Who in their right mind would invite a girl back for tea to our house?

And then we move.

Grandpa Percy and grandma Clara are what will in a couple of decades be called 'downsizing.' Not that 2 Tofts Road, Cleckheaton is of mansion-like proportions. It's a commonplace Edwardian two-up two-down end-of-terrace. Bow-window at the front, small extension kitchen at the back, and −as we recall − the bathroom where I was indulged as an infant! Apparently, they have agreed to sell it to my mother and Fred. It will mean a much longer journey for me to school, but I will have a proper room at least − albeit shared with Ian. Both Fred and my mother can get jobs nearby. Percy and Clara will be 'just up the road,' so I'll have somewhere close by to get away.

Fairly soon after my sixteenth birthday we make the move. It's refreshing to have − relatively − so much room. And my God, at last, to be able to go to the loo inside! And take a bath! And cook in a kitchen with a proper sink with hot and cold water! There's even a small back yard; useful for repairing my bike. If *he* weren't here, it would be heaven!

The trip to and from school is a chore, though. Where it used to take about ten minutes on my first bus into Halifax centre, it now takes around an hour. I can at least use Alice's house as a temporary stopover after school. Her − also Edwardian − terraced house is possibly even smaller than 12 Shibden Fold. It too has an outside toilet, but it's adjacent to the house, and has a flush! She has to cook on a gas stove at the bottom of the cellar steps, which run directly down from a door to the living room, and at the top of which is just room for a sink. It's sparse, but comfy. When I stay, which is not often, I'm in a sleeping bag on the living-room floor.

At Tofts Road, inevitably, the novelty-induced calm of being in the bigger house soon wears off, and things become fractious again. It's not easy for a teenage boy, sharing a room with his four-year-old half-brother, and living in a constant state of mutual contempt with an overbearing step-father.

The situation grows increasingly untenable, until finally, inevitably, it erupts. An argument over the usual inconsequentialities flares up between me and Fred. My mother intervenes, Fred has a go at her – verbally, but it's looking as though it's going to get a bit violent. Although I've never seen him strike her, he seems often on the verge. My hormones take over; I step between them. Fred lunges at me, and from nowhere, I deliver the second of my life's two uppercuts.

It's not bad, considering: perfectly timed and executed, and lands right on the point of his jaw, snapping his head back.

Unfortunately, I'm not muscular, especially being only just sixteen. I'm nowhere near as tall or as heavy as he, and my blow results only in repelling him a few inches. A look of total shock and disbelief transfixes his face. But this lasts only a second. He regains his balance, and with that look I know so well, he's coming at me. History repeats, and I'm off. I spin and crash out of the living room, then through the front door and into the street. It's all so familiar. This time, though, there are crucial differences. I'm afraid, yes; I've been afraid of him for so long, my DNA has adjusted to incorporate it, but there's also an undeniably jubilant feeling of 'I did it!" I hit him!' The fear does not have such a paralysing control over me. So, once outside, I stop and turn. I keep enough distance to escape if need be – he's still a big, strong bloke – but I have enough guts to shout at him "You bastard!" You f------ bastard! That's it, I'm leaving!" "Good riddance!" is of course the response, but stand-off or not, chased out of the house or not, I have a strange, almost out-of-body sense of triumph. Somewhere inside I know that, marginal though my victory is, things can never be the same again. Not just that I will now have to move out – much to my mother's

History of a Daft A'porth

distress – but that from now on, as I grow undeniably stronger, he will grow correspondingly weaker. One day, there will be no more running away. One day, in the not too distant future, I know, and I can see in his eyes that he does too, that if he tries it on again, I will knock him down, and he won't want to get up.

Right now, I arrange with my mother and grandmother for me to go and live at Alice's until we can – in my mother's words – 'sort things out.'

We don't sort things out. We can't. My mother won't admit it to herself, but everyone knows. I'll stay at my grandmother's until I go to university, and despite my mother's pleas, I will never move back into that house.

It's quite an adjustment for my gran, whom I now address as Alice, me being all grown-up-and-left-home, and all. After a while she stops objecting to the use of her name, and it becomes normal between us. It's one of the changes I've foisted upon her by my precipitous departure from the family home. These changes include: me on a single bed crammed into her miniscule bedroom; watching Doctor Who or The Forsyte Saga with her on her little TV; she cooking and cleaning for me (I do help occasionally!) and my coming home from evenings in the pub not infrequently a little the worse for wear. At moments like these as I collapse into an armchair with the room swirling giddily around me, and trying not to throw up on her carpet, she exudes that curious mixture of sympathy and opprobrium that only grandparents seem able to convey.

Generally, the arrangement works out. A lasting regret for me, unfortunately, will be that the pent-up resentment towards Fred that I have inside me manifests itself more than once in displays of vile bad temper towards Alice. This is undoubtedly augmented by teenage hormones, but even so, it's totally unjustifiable, and I will always look back on it with shame. I upset her terribly, many, many times.

Alice – my mother's mother – has always played an important part in my life. As a pre-school child, with my mother at work during the day, Alice, and Louis, my grandad, were my safe havens to whom I would steer my battered little ship during the multitude of tiny tempests that beset a child of that age. The splinter incident being such a storm.

She and Louis met in Kenya (when it was pronounced Keen-ya). She was working as an auxiliary nurse; he was a music-hall-style entertainer. He played piano and sang popular songs, mostly in concerts to the British troops billeted there at the time; the boot of colonialism being still, at the time, firmly on Africa's neck. He was also, he would later claim to me, a whiz at snooker and billiards – a talent I sadly never inherited. They lived near Nairobi, and my Mother, Emily, was born there in 1928. As Europeans they were privileged enough, even with their modest income, to have a maid: a local Kikuyu woman, who looked after Emily, and whom she loved dearly. My mother proudly claims, when occasion merits, that, on the family's return to England when Emily was four, thanks to that maid, she was fluent in Swahili, and hardly spoke a word of English. I take this with a very large pinch of salt, but she remains adamant. As an adult she can only remember a few words: Simba – lion; hapana – no; ndio – yes. The rest is gone.

They establish a life in London. Through the thirties, they survive the crash, and watch with dread the rise of Nazi Germany. They live through the Blitz. As a boy, I thrill to the doodlebug story. One of these 'Victory Weapons' of Hitler's landed close to their house one night, turfing the teenage Emily out of her bed, and simultaneously dumping the nearby massive marble dresser top onto the spot where a second before, she had been sleeping.

There are other stories too; back in Kenya, shaking shoes in the morning, to dislodge any lethal snakes who had made them their overnight bed; in Halifax, Alice's father, known to all as 'Pop,' calming then leading panicked dray horses out of a runaway fire at the brewery where he worked; her formidable Victorian mother-in-law, who forbade her to speak unless spoken to, and once slapped across the face for 'cheek.'

And then there are the people she 'sees'.

History of a Daft A'porth

This is a difficult side of Alice for me, increasingly so for me as an adult. Since I was tiny, she has spoken of her 'visitors.' These were not the folk who were invited into the hallowed Front Room, although they were often the reason those friends and acquaintances were there. My grandmother is a practising spiritualist. Not only is she a member of the movement, she claims to be a medium.

Mediums do not have a stain-free history, to say the least. Revered in ancient times, burned as witches during the inquisition, and a source of heated intellectual, moral, and scientific controversy for the Victorians. Many have, of course, been revealed as psychotic, deluded, or fraudsters; some raking fortunes from the gullible rich, perpetrating elaborate scams on huge numbers of the public, and artfully gulling prominent figures – Sir Arthur Conan Doyle being probably the most famous. So, it can't be said the spiritualist movement has garnered a particularly positive image. Since those hysterical eras, things have calmed down, however, and the movement is now regarded as a kind of slightly batty fringe religion, its practitioners still rather suspect – on a par with fortune tellers and American life-gurus.

But Alice is my gran; very ordinary, and seems as far removed from these charlatans and madmen as it is possible to get. As a small child, I was used to her talking occasionally about her 'spirit guides,' and the 'people' she claims to see and talk with. It seemed every-day to me. Then we moved away, and for the next few years, I rarely saw her. We came back to Halifax, and I would visit more often, but it's only when I move in with her permanently that I really begin to struggle with the contradictions. When my grandad Louis died in 1959, Alice couldn't keep 10 York Terrace, and was allocated the small terraced council house where she now lives, in Coton St, in the west of the town. The Shay rugby ground, where Halifax Town play, is near enough to hear the sea-swell of the crowd roaring and groaning on a Saturday afternoon. It's at the little red front door of this house that I wash up, aged sixteen, having punched my stepfather, and fled the coop.

She has never tried to mystify her spiritualism. On the odd occasion 'they' visit when we are together in the house, she speaks of the faces and voices as though they've just popped in from next door for a cup of tea, or to return a borrowed book. She'll sometimes nod in agreement, or tell them to "Shush, just a minute," or "Hang on a tick." It's all so... ordinary! She travels all over the county to meetings, for which she's paid expenses and a small fee. There's not the slightest possibility that she's making money out of it. This is emphatically *not* a scam. She's as poor as the rest of our family. As a teenage boy, I don't really know what to make of it. I've grown up with it being a 'normal,' if peripheral, part of my life. My mother seems to take it for granted, and I've never felt the need to challenge it. Even now, I would not be comfortable doing so. In a way, I want it to be real. I want it all to be true. Partly because the fairly pedestrian life after death as she describes it doesn't seem like an altogether bad idea (personally, I've never been keen on the harps-and-hymns-for-eternity version), but also, because I don't want my gran to turn out to be bonkers. So I've always accepted it in an unprotesting, unchallenging way. When I go away to university, I leave the dichotomy behind. Out of sight, out of mind.

Except for one occasion. One of my mates in the student house I move into is persuaded by his girlfriend that there is a 'presence' in their bedroom; a coldness, and a feeling of 'someone being there.' It's not terrifying, but she's sufficiently unnerved to ask for help. The prevailing cultural atmosphere of the early seventies – especially amongst students – is one of spiritual exploration and open-ness to pretty much any idea of mind beyond body, no matter how far-fetched, whacky, or unlikely. "There are more things in heaven and earth than are dreamed of in your philosophy, Horatio," and so on. Still ambivalent about the whole afterlife thing, I call in my elite troops to reassure the household. Alice comes over to Sheffield in her role as consulting expert. Entering the bedroom in question, she concurs that there is something there, but after some internal discussion, she assures us it's unthreatening, and tells us not to worry. We, rational, scientific, modern, intellectual thinkers,

History of a Daft A'porth

just accept all of this, and we all go down for tea. Alice goes home the following day, and after a while, we forget about it entirely. In later life I can only conclude that Alice's mundane inclusion of the spirit world into her everyday life, plus the hippy-dippy student philosophies in which we were immersed, served only to delay my eventual and inevitable conversion to agnostic. Not atheist, because as my future brother-in law will correctly point out, one can never be completely sure either way! This conversion will be hastened along after Alice's death in 1980. Occasionally, and for years afterwards, I will lie in the dark before sleep, silently pleading with her to make herself known, to prove it was all true, whilst knowing in my heart there will be *no* reply from beyond; the end is the end. The only rational conclusion I can reach about her beliefs, is that she suffered her entire life from some kind of hallucinations or delusions. Fortunately, they didn't seem to impinge on other aspects of her or our life, and certainly they didn't prevent me from loving her.

Although in the first few months of living with her now, I make her life hell with my teenage temper!

It comes as a great relief to us both when, after a few months, I undergo what I can only describe as some sort of epiphany. It may be that the stress of previous home life has at last eased; I suddenly realise what I am doing, and even – with a rare burst of maturity – why I'm doing it, and everything rapidly gets better between us. Like magic, the arguments cease. I settle into sixth form, and start to live what I feel for the first time in my life, is a normal existence.

And I have a girlfriend! Her name is Pat, she's my age, darkhaired, smart, voluptuously pretty, and like Ash, she goes to Crossley and Porter school.

Which is how we met. Ash and Pat know each other through school, and she sometimes comes to the coffee bar. It was here that he introduced us, and we would flirt, fluorescing brightly at one another under the UV lights.

I've never asked a girl out before, and I make the conventional adolescent fumbling attempt, but amazingly, she accepts. We arrange to meet in a couple of days.

I can't believe it, the first time I've dared to ask a girl out, and she's said yes!

I take her to the fair that has recently set up in its brassy, insistent annual visit on a patch of waste ground at the edge of the town. I'm hoping it will be more original than the cinema! She seems to think so, and is happily animated as we wander through the attractions. We decide our first ride will be the Waltzer. Oh, quelle erreur! Have I have so easily forgotten my experiences of motion sickness in the Air Cadets or as a motorbike pillion? The cars whirl and spin at high speed around a track that also undulates vigorously up and down (not unlike like a light aircraft!) Not only this, but at regular intervals, one of the ride attendants clamps himself onto the outside of the car, and uses his mass, along with an expert grasp of the principle of conservation of momentum, to temporarily and radically increase its rotational speed. Pat loves it, but it takes all my will power not to throw up all over her. Mercifully, I make it to the end of the ride. Just. After this, I very carefully steer her away from any similar perils, and we spend a lot of time either on the dodgems, or with me showing off my marksmanship, winning her sizeable, if cheap and gaudy, fluffy toys on the rifle ranges. The weather's warm and dry, the crowds are noisily cheerful, we enjoy each other's company, and despite my almost disaster on the Waltzer, the evening goes well. As in all fairgrounds before and since, there's loud music blasted out at high volume on all sides. Each stall or ride has its own multi-decibel accompaniment competing with all the others. Gone are the days of the pipe-organ powered by the ride's mechanism, whistling and fluting its music-hall favourites; everyone here has their own high-power PA, and the music from each is almost exclusively Motown. Every recent hit is played over and over at different moments in different parts of the fairground. In later years, just the briefest snatch of The Supremes' *Baby Love*, or Smokey Robinson's *The Tracks of my Tears*, or any other song

History of a Daft A'porth

from that period's canon, will transport me instantly and vividly back to that marvellous evening wandering the fairground eating candyfloss, surrounded by pounding music and screams of delight in every direction, the smell of hot dogs, whirling lights and machinery, and holding hands with Pat.

After the fair, in true gentlemanly fashion I escort her home, and I have my first ever kiss, which chastely takes place in true traditional style, on her doorstep, saying goodnight. It is as wonderful as I could have hoped: tender, soft, and lasting.

She's an occasional smoker, offering me one whenever she lights up. I always refuse politely. Fred smokes. That, plus the detestable mixed odour of cigarettes and urine in the toilets at school, cause me to abstain – until I finally and foolishly cave in at university. When Pat and I kiss, I can taste the cigarettes on her breath. Oddly, I find it not unpleasant. It's only a slight tobacco hint, mingled with the mints she uses to mitigate it when she gets home, and I'm not put off at all. It's far removed from the awful, repellent, old-ashtray taste on the breath of heavy-smoking girls I will occasionally kiss in later escapades. Pat and I will kiss reasonably often, but you couldn't call it snogging. Snogging is yet to be discovered.

In fact, as romances go, Romeo and Juliet it is not. We're more like an old married couple, affectionate and amiable, but not passionate. This is not love's young dream. It doesn't even flash and fade like the proverbial shooting star. Pat and I are boyfriend and girlfriend in an almost fraternal way. I'm a sixteen-year-old heterosexual male; it's not that I don't want to have a more intimate relationship. I've suffered the usual lack of intimate information from responsible adults that is common at this period, but as a thirteen-year-old I spent quite a bit of time in the school library before anybody else got to school, clandestinely soaking up the human reproduction sections of the relevant textbooks. Over the years, I've also managed to sift the important biological truths from the braggadocio and self-aggrandising fantasy of my schoolmates. I am thus sufficiently well-informed to participate at least competently in the act of union. And I would certainly like to. But for me and Pat, it never happens. I think I am just too gentlemanly to suggest it, and – whatever her reasons – she never drops any hints either. The relationship, if we can call it that, doesn't last, and we part amicably. Despite my subsequently and serially trying for a more intimate relationship, with other girls, it will be another three years before I finally and painfully discover that, in the words of rock gods Nazareth: *Love Hurts*. Until then, for me, it just *hides*.

In the intervening years, I will have crushes on various girls, some of whom will graciously agree to go out with me. One or two will even turn up as agreed! However, my attempts at intimacy will be hampered by a persistent lack of self-confidence (it will take the loving – and I hope, objective – insistence of eventual long-term partners to convince me I'm not unpleasant to look at), and by a terror of teenage pregnancy. Until I get to university, I'll experience neither the breath-taking rush of passion, nor the sticky accompaniments of its physical expression. I am what in my mature years I'll look back on with a great deal of sympathy: a 'late developer.' Although it does me no lasting harm, this involuntary solitude is a consistent source of sadness and frustration, and will often recur in later years. Perhaps I'm looking for a kind of stability to replace that which I've never felt at home – who knows? Whatever the cause, I will remain, always, someone who is most content within a relationship, and always more melancholy from the lack of one. To describe the way it works or doesn't work, I call on more wise words: as the Supremes succinctly point out, *You Can't Hurry Love*.

My mother has made a decision. She's been in touch with the Benson side of the family, and it's all been thoroughly discussed. I'm sixteen, and it's high time I met Derrick – my father. I'm ambivalent about the news. He's done little, if anything, to support me since they divorced, and I've only ever seen his face in photographs. On the one hand, I agree with my mother: it's been far too long, and we are strangers to each other. On the other, for much the same reasons, it's a bit terrifying. What if we

History of a Daft A'porth

don't get on? What if he turns out to be a similar sort of ogre to Fred? What if, what if... Summoning a modicum of maturity, I agree to the encounter (I have at least been given the choice!) It's decided that this historic event should take place at my grandparents' (Percy and Clara's) house. On the day, my mother and I wait, fidgeting, in their sitting room. There's a knock at the front door, which my grandmother Clara answers. I hear an exchange of greetings and pecks on the cheek, the door to the sitting room opens, and in comes my father.

It's very strange, meeting a person, in one way so intimately attached to your life, and yet so thoroughly distanced from it. I find myself struggling to balance a powerful feeling of curiosity with one of enormous resentment at having been abandoned; especially, abandoned to a bully. All of these feelings are swirling around inside me as Derrick walks in, and I have to deal with the present moment.

My father is tall, slim, and youthfully good looking. He turns out to be unexpectedly warm, animated, and interesting, and he has a way of listening and encouraging me to talk that slowly begins to open a connection between us. It's tenuous, but there's definitely something there. We chat about our lives; he tells me of his work abroad, his home in Doncaster, and his second wife, Rene. I talk about school, rugby, my hobbies, friends, and so-on. My mother offers the occasional comment; most of it thinly veiled sniping at Derrick's lack of support. After not very long at all, we seem to be getting on quite well. I will later be told by more than one person, just how alike we are, my father and I. Perhaps that's why we manage, despite all the odds, to strike up a relationship right from the start. The time comes for him to leave, and we arrange for me to go and stay for a weekend.

That weekend arrives, and I catch the bus to Doncaster. Derrick has offered to meet me at the bus station, and we drive in his Morris Traveller estate car to his house in the – to me – rather posh area of Wheatley, just outside the town centre. We're welcomed at the door by Rene. She's older than I'd expected; tall, dark, with a slightly eastern European air, and is incredibly nervous – far more than I. Despite this, she and I fall for each other almost immediately. She is incredibly warm, generous, affectionate, and chatty. Sadly, she's also a very heavy smoker, and her cough is terrifying. I also later learn from Derrick, that she's unable to have children, which may go some way to explaining how fond of me she becomes. Right from the start she can't do enough for me; food, trips out, little gifts, a cake to take away when I leave; all are offered with an obviously open and kindly heart. My father and I spend more time catching up, and all in all, it's a happy weekend.

There is just one moment when it all nearly falls apart. On the second day, Derrick admonishes me for 'elbows on the table' at dinner. It's exactly the sort of pointless regulation I have to endure from Fred. My reflex is to walk out. To my credit, though, I swallow my bile, keep a straight face, and comply without comment. I keep the fury inside me invisible, and it subsides. Calm returns. I suspect Derrick has realised his error, and I'm never criticised in that way again. The moment passes without incident, and for that I will be eternally thankful. Had I allowed the anger inside me to surface, I would never have had the joy of a lasting relationship with my father, with Rene, and eventually, with his third partner, Dorothy. Nor would he have had the delight of seeing his baby grand-daughters playing at his feet.

I will continue to visit, sometimes with my girlfriend of the moment, and will enjoy many happy hours in Derrick's company, listening to tales of my grandpa Percy, which my father relates with such verve and humour they have us in stitches. Rene and I will become so close she'll be like a second mum to me. So much so, that a few short years later, when she dies suddenly of the lung cancer brought on by her heavy smoking, I shall be devastated. Poor Derrick is stricken with a profound and debilitating grief. When I see him a few weeks after the funeral, (to which I am unable go), he looks ten years older, emptied of all his vigour, broken, and lost. I've never seen this kind of grief before, and I don't know how to speak to him. Although we will keep in touch in the coming years, I don't visit as much, not least because I'm working now, so less able to get away. It will be a long time before I will see him happy again.

History of a Daft A'porth

During the first weeks of reconciliation with Derrick, I come to the end of my lower sixth year, spend a summer vacation working on the dustbins, and in September 1968, launch into the upper sixth.

This is where things get serious. We layabouts now realise that we have to get down to some proper work. The lower sixth was a haze of new social life, lessons interspersed with indolent free periods, bossing the lower school around in our new roles as prefects, and lots of running up and down stairs for rugby training. The upper sixth is pretty much the same... but with lots more work thrown in. We've all made our applications to university, and what we have to do now is get the A-level grades required. I'm talking physics, maths, chemistry and general studies. Physics is something I've always enjoyed, it appeals to the engineer in me (do I get that from my father?) – all that electricity, magnetism, gravity, etc; and Howard Wroot is a scream. As well as regular visits from Frank, the biology room polecat with a taste for leg hair, our lab is filled with flashing strobes, bouncing table tennis balls, humming wires, and *Outer-Limits*-like oscilloscope screens. Helpfully, the maths needed is relatively simple.

Pure maths, thanks to its obvious relation to physics, I find manageable, but occasionally baffling. Not so baffling that I can't do it – I get it eventually – but baffling in the manner of why would you ever need to do this? I'm obviously not cut out to be a pure mathematician. Maths is a language in which I can get by, but its higher vocabulary and grammar will remain forever beyond my reach. Future insights, usually gained through TV documentaries or biopic movies, will show me that you have to be a very special kind of person to speak pure maths. I'm definitely not that kind of person.

Chemistry is worse. Why, oh why, did I pick chemistry? The inorganic stuff is reasonably straightforward – again, a fair amount of simple maths and some laws to remember, but the organic side! So many hydrocarbons! And all so confusingly similar. It's like trying to put together a jigsaw puzzle where the pieces barely differ in shape, and are all the same colour. I do not enjoy it in the slightest. Only a great deal of grindingly boring revision and some luck in the questions allow me to scrape the exam.

It's in general studies – a recently added subject option – that I'm truly happy. It covers a range of subjects from social history through literature and philosophy to psychology, and I thoroughly enjoy it. Its broad approach and "grown-up" syllabus give me a taste of the wider world, a world that's increasingly beginning to impinge on our circumscribed little lives.

And cloistered though may be, we *are* beginning to take note. Since 1964, we've had a labour government for the first time in my life. My family (both branches) have always been working class Tories. I well remember my grandmother talking with huge pride about the then prime minister, Harold MacMillan, and his famous *You've never had it so good* speech, and her dislike of all Labour politicians. I'm not in agreement. This is the birth of my political awareness. It's on very shallow foundations, I'm not well-informed on political subjects, but I have my highly developed sense of fair-play, and I cannot believe that the Tory party, with its old-boy network and land-owning members of parliament, can possibly represent my parents and grandparents and the other working people of this country. I'm even more perplexed by the support and deference this elite receives from my family. My beliefs are simple, but I hold them firmly, and they will later be fleshed out by my studies and experiences at and after university. For now, at least, part of the real world has filtered into the cocooned environment of school and home. The world has a habit of doing this in the most tragic of ways, as the United States has again just made plain with the assassination of Martin Luther King in June. Shockingly, he will be followed only six months later by Bobbie Kennedy, Jack's brother. Politically (and generally) naïve that we still are, these events, though shocking, have a more emotional than global significance for us. I won't understand their true historical moment, as an attack on equality, freedom, and progress, until I become embroiled in the hothouse of debate that is university life.

History of a Daft A'porth

1969 arrives, shortly followed by my eighteenth birthday. I've chosen my universities, and have set myself to revise frantically between now and my A-levels.

The year turns to a balmy spring and summer. I spend a lot of revision time outside, lying in the sun reading my notes and text books, and doing my practice essays. As a result, I get horribly sunburned, pass an unpleasantly painful couple of days peeling like an old silver birch, but carry on working. I have to pass! I cannot contemplate having to get a job in a factory or an office instead of going to uni. Even my social life is curtailed. I'm not going to the pub as often with my mates, and, though not for want of trying, I haven't had a girlfriend for months. I surprise myself with my application to work, but that doesn't save me from viewing the approaching exam period with some trepidation.

Crunch time arrives, and day after day, subject after subject, the lambs file dutifully into the hall, and then out (some out sooner than others, to be sick, or fleeing the stress). Somehow or another I make it to the end of the two weeks of torture 'intact,' if not exactly brimming with confidence. Done my best. Can't do any more. It's over!

I've one last thing to achieve before the summer break.

In his town hall office in Halifax, I explain to the registrar behind his impressive desk, that I wish to change my surname by deed poll. I've researched it, and this seems the best method. There's a fee to pay, but I'm so determined to rid myself of the patronymic millstone around my neck, that I would pay any cost. The registrar asks if I have a passport. Hearing that I don't, he suggests I simply rely on what is termed 'use and reputation.' Deed poll isn't legally necessary. In other words, If I *say* my name is 'such-and-such,' it *is* 'such-and-such.' I get to dump the name that has such a loathsome taste in my mouth, and even better, for free! I won't need to change my birth certificate, as I was only saddled with Fred's surname at the age of five. I will henceforth return to my infant surname of 'Benson.'

I feel as if I've had iron manacles removed from my arms and legs.

Term comes to an end, and with it, my school life. Because of my frequent decamping from one primary school to the next, saying goodbye to friends hasn't, before now, been hard for me. This time, it is. I've been with most of this lot for seven years, through times of fundamental change. Strong bonds are formed in these circumstances, but even these will fray and part with distance and time. People fill a similar role to topographical landmarks in one's life. We navigate around, sometimes bumping into, these almost omnipresent features of our universe – often taken for granted until they begin to recede into the distance at the start of a journey. We think we'll never forget them, but just like the buildings and the landscapes we leave behind, unless we revisit them often they begin to fade in our memories. So it is with my school friends. I've worked, played, laughed with, and shed the occasional tear alongside them, but just as I've lost the names and faces of most from my infancy, few of these schoolmates from Halifax will remain vivid or even present in my thoughts after a few decades. The period over the summer break is the last I'll spend time with any of them: some work on the bins with me for a while, but one by one, they leave for work or college. It is – as they say – the end of an era. Writing this, many decades hence, I will have to call upon the utmost efforts of memory to bring them back out of the mists, to see their shining schoolboy features once again. Leaving friends behind seems to be a recurring theme in my life.

Finally, results time comes around. The world holds its breath.

History of a Daft A'porth

Chapter 7: Sex 'n Drugs 'n Rock and Roll?

> Turn, turn, my wheel! 'Tis nature's plan
> The child should grow into the man,
> > Henry Wadsworth Longfellow
> > The Song of the Potter

I got my grades! Sheffield has offered me a place! I'm going to university! First in the family, and all that.
Sex 'n Drugs 'n Rock and Roll, here I come!

Except it's not quite that easy. Certainly not at the beginning.
The idea of Sex 'n Drugs 'n Rock and Roll is not even fully formed in my mind at this age. Yes, of course I know what those things are, but my experience of them has so far been rudimentary, fumbling, and unfulfilled in every sense.
I arrive at university straight from my very working-class very conservative (both small and large 'C'), racist, sexist, homophobic, and culturally barren background, sporting an early mop-top haircut, a blazer, and what can only be described as mildly flared slacks. All around me on this modernist, square-blocked, forward-thrusting campus, are people who look – and for the little that I know, behave – like Eric Clapton or Joni Mitchell; and having only recently heard their names, I don't yet really know who these presumed idols are! O brave new world...!
For a day or so, I wander wide-eyed and awestruck around the students' union, a fish out of water, until the rather obvious penny drops. I have to do something. It can't be hard; Sheffield city is well prepared for eager ingenues like me. There is a multitude of well stocked 'head' shops selling everything the aspiring hippy could ever need. I buy proper flares (denim; super wide), a couple of skinny T-shirts and an ex-army jacket, and my hair begins its slow progression to cavalier length. It won't see a pair of scissors for almost a year – only slightly less time than my new beard and moustache. Slacks and blazer – in the bin!

Thus, I join the tribe, in theory at least. As for Sex 'n Drugs 'n Rock and Roll, well, I discover those pretty much in reverse order...

Rock and Roll...

All first-year students not living in their family home are obliged to live either in a hall of residence or digs. I'm in shared digs chez Mrs Bodsworth, a bus-ride or two way from the campus. Mrs Bodsworth is very nice, quite motherly, and not too strict... the usual: don't be noisy, no coming in drunk, no girls (as if...!) etc, and for our entertainment she has a crazy kamikaze budgie that keeps flying into the washing machine.

For a while, everything's fine. The week before term starts is Freshers' Week, and as at all universities, it's a frenzy of registrations, exploring campus and town, buying books (which inevitably turn out to be the wrong ones), checking out societies, and figuring out who will be your mates. The number and scope of societies is vast, and frankly, my interests are so circumscribed by my upbringing that I don't feel inclined at this point to join any of them. I am slightly intimidated by the obviously superior worldliness and confidence of their members, so I wander aimlessly through the students' union searching for reasons to be there. No friends as yet; you make acquaintances all the time, in queues mostly; waiting your turn in the refectory at lunchtime; lining up to register for your courses; reading messages on the student board outside the porters' lodge. It will be a while before there's any message left for me, but those currently up there make fascinating and baffling reading.

"Tom Redcliffe: Bus late. sorry. Toblerone, 6 tonite."
"Porky: Just don't!"
"Has anyone seen Charlie?"

No wiser, I drift two floors downstairs to the bar. It's around one pm, and it's packed. Thus far, I know not a soul, and continue through to the back area where the games rooms are. Sheffield

History of a Daft A'porth

students' union is relatively well off: alongside a spacious bar area, it boasts a snooker room with two full size, well-maintained tables, and further on, I discover, a table tennis room with four tables. As I enter this room, out of simple curiosity, a strange theatre is in progress. About half a dozen blokes of my age, holding bats, are careering wildly around the nearest table like demented circus ponies, frantically trying to keep the ball going back and forth over the net as they run. They're not having much success, and there are frequent collapses into helpless laughter as the ball careens off in all directions but the one desired. Not a lot of success, but obviously a lot of fun. During one of these brief but hysterical pauses, I feel a bat thrust into my hand, and all of a sudden, I am part of this mad rampage, slashing wildly at the little white sphere, and occasionally managing to get it over the net. More often than not, it strikes one of the 'players,' in the head, and we all dissolve into heaving giggles like three-year-olds on a bouncy castle.

This game continues until we're all exhausted and come to a stop, snorting with residual laughter, and panting like cattle after a stampede. Who are these people!?

These people – all newbies like me – plus some with whom they room, attend lectures, or fall in love, will become some of my closest and dearest friends, whose companionship will last the whole of our university careers. With some, it will continue beyond, and with one or two, it will still be strong as I write this book, and hopefully after that. I seem to have found my gang.

Having mates changes everything. Digs will no longer do! The students' union or the halls of residence are where it's at, man! Having to catch the bus back to Mrs Bodsworth's every night becomes intolerable. I stay the night occasionally on someone's floor in Ranmoor or Hallam or some other hall of residence, or I roll into Mrs B's at two in the morning. She does *not* approve. Something has to give. So, at the end of the first term, I announce that I won't be lodging with her at the beginning of the next. She, despite my bad behaviour, is not best pleased.

Students are supposed to stay in their assigned accommodation for the full year. The university goes to a lot of trouble to find these lodgings, and we should all be suitably grateful! 'I am!' I protest.

Am I, though, really? I'm moving out, regardless.

Although I expect repercussions, surprisingly there are none, and at the start of the next term, along with six of my mates who have taken similar nonconformist routes, I move into a house fifteen minutes' walk from the main university buildings. It's number twelve on a small cul-de-sac called the Nook. These are the beginnings of the Nook years.

We're two Andy's, one Chris, one Bob, one Keith, a Ges, and me. It's a big house, if a little tatty. Keith and I share a room.

Keith is funny, smart, and interesting. He's studying dentistry, a discipline which, from his description, seems to involve an inordinate amount of time and effort compared to the rest of us. It's he who will really open my ears and my mind to rock and roll. (He'll also eventually abandon dentistry to become a nurse.) My experience of music thus far is limited to the ownership of two early albums by that now rather more famous band – now returned from Hamburg – and hearing Pink Floyd's album *Piper at the Gates of Dawn* in the sixth form common room – brought in and played by a boy whom no one seemed to like very much. DJ I am not.

Keith, on the other hand, already possesses a fine collection of LPs and a vast knowledge of bands, tracks and lyrics. I'm rather awe-struck, and more than a little jealous of the cachet this bestows on him. Intrigued, I go with him and some of the others to my first live rock band.

Sheffield Students' Union is large enough to be a significant venue for touring bands, and big names at that. My first is not one of the real greats such as The Who or Cream, whom I'll see later. My unreliable memory of it in the future will insist it was John Heisman's Colosseum, whom we see so many times over the years that they achieve the status almost of a resident band at Sheffield. So they *may* not be the first band I see live, but they *probably* are!

History of a Daft A'porth

My first live rock band! As a schoolboy I sat and listened dutifully to jazz trios in the pubs in Halifax, because I thought I should, but nothing so tame could have prepared me for this explosion of the senses. I'm – almost literally – blown away. When we leave, my ears are ringing, and I can't stop raving about Heisman's drum solos, or Heckstall–Smith's incredible saxophone. My life will never be the same.

Over the next few months, I see every band I can, without discrimination, gradually refining my knowledge and tastes until I know who's worth seeing – or where I can find this out. I shamelessly borrow LPs from better-off friends who can afford to buy them, and record them on my big reel-to reel tape machine. By these rather devious means, I eventually have a "borrowed" collection far more extensive than that of any of my selfless mates, but I try at least to make it up to them by throwing endless parties at the Nook, as we now call the house itself.

Because of Sheffield's popularity as a venue, we see some real legends live; The Who and Cream, as mentioned, T Rex, John Mayall, Traffic, Led Zeppelin, Free, Jethro Tull, and a stream of rock legends, (including Roxy Music for 50p[1], who have just become famous, and were pre-booked!). Further exploration via my more eclectic friends leads me to a host of other-genre bands; Fairport Convention, Pentangle, The Incredible String Band, Bonzo Dog Doo Da Band, The Byrds, and scores of others, as well as traditional folk at the union folk club. The high-point of this voyage of discovery comes in September 1970, when– along with a few thousand other anointed – Bob and I attend the first-ever Glastonbury festival.

We hitch-hike with little difficulty from Sheffield to Worthy Farm. And the festival is truly amazing, like nothing I've ever seen: so many people! Most wearing beads, and some – it being hot – not much else; a sea of tents, a fog of marihuana over the entire site, crazy, stoned dancing, and open toilets that remind me disquietingly of my childhood in Shibden Fold. Miraculously,

---

[1] *Around £7.00 in 2021*

unlike future Glasto's, the weather stays dry and warm for the whole time. The line-up is equally unforgettable. Our main problem is staying awake for the late-night bands. To my chagrin, I wake on the third morning to find that I've slept through Pink Floyd. I am gutted, as they're my favourite band! Fortunately, I will make up this loss, seeing them live subsequently at least half a dozen times. I don't hang on to my disappointment: there are dozens of great bands left in the line-up, and we have a ball! Sadly, it comes to an end, and along with thousands of other exhausted but elated people, Bob and I pack the tent, and set out to hitch home.

Going back proves to be not so easy. We walk for eight solid, hot and dispiriting hours out of Shepton Mallet, our thumbs working overtime, without a single soul offering us a lift. It's utterly demoralizing. And then the universe delivers one of those capricious little surprises that it can drop into your life with a self-satisfied smirk!

We drag ourselves into Box – a village outside Bath – at around six pm, and decide that, useless as our thumbs have proven to be, we will rest them overnight, sleep in the village bus-shelter, and

take up the slog the following day. Before turning in, though, we've earned a pie and a pint or two. We stagger, exhausted, into the first pub we come to. Over a first glass of the excellent local brew, and said pie, we strike up a conversation with the very convivial regulars, eventually join their game of darts, and spend a thoroughly enjoyable evening losing over and over again but enjoying the company, laughing and chatting. Naturally, we enlarge upon our adventure of the last few days and its depressing last few hours on the road. When pressed, we reveal our plans for sleeping in the bus-shelter. Oh, they will have none of it! Almost falling over each other, they offer help: garden sheds, front-room couches, etc. One of them finally wins the day, offering me and Bob – unkempt, long-haired, rucksack laden, and doubtlessly not terribly floral – a bed for the night, and a bath. Astonished and not a little moved, we accept, and at

History of a Daft A'porth

closing time we bid a boozy farewell to the others, and accompany our benefactor back to his nearby house.

His wife, apparently not in the least taken aback when he marches in with us and gushes out our predicament, welcomes us with matching hospitality. We join them for supper, have a bath, and are given the spare room, where we can share the double bed. In the morning, after his wife makes us a hearty breakfast, the husband drives us the twelve miles to the nearest M4 junction – "So you'll have a better chance of a lift." It's one of those moments where one's faith in human nature, so often eroded by cruelty, indifference or selfishness, is comprehensively restored. As Bob and I watch our hero's car disappear down the road, we're both on the verge of tears after the spontaneous, unsolicited generosity we have just received.

Back home again, musically, a void has been filled, I'm a more complete human being. I'm eternally grateful to Keith and all the other friends who've contributed their knowledge (and their albums!). I now know all about music!

Well...no, actually, not *all* about it...

It's one afternoon in August. Keith is off soon to a lecture, and I'm at a loose end, slouched on the floor between the two huge tower speakers of the stereo in our room, doing nothing in particular.

D'you know this?" Keith asks. He shows me the album cover. I shrug.

"Nope."

"You should listen to it,"

"Oh yeah?".

"Yeah."

"OK."

He sets it up on the stereo, nods at me, and leaves for his class. The door closes behind him, and the opening bars of Tchaikovsky's Violin Concerto in D Major wash over me.

Fifteen minutes later there are tears pouring down my face: I'm transfixed by emotion. Never in my life has a piece of music had this effect on me. I had no idea it could do this.

We 'did' Tchaikovsky in music lessons at school, along with the other greats – basic bio, main pieces, etc, and I had a vague idea that he hadn't lived the happiest of lives, but this...!
So much pain, so much heartache. How can one human being communicate *so directly* to another's heart, simply by some dots scrawled on a paper and the drawing of a bow across four strings? By the end of the piece I'm wrecked, but transported. From now on I shall explore the world of classical music as avidly as that of rock. The final doors have been opened, and the coming years will see my musical tastes expand rapidly to embrace every genre; rock folk, country and western, jazz, African, Indian, Latin, ballad, heavy metal, punk, etc, etc – yes, eventually even the occasional rap or hip hop!
What category it falls into isn't relevant...
As Louis Armstrong allegedly said, "There is two kinds of music; the good and the bad."

Good or bad, music fills up an enormous part of our lives and thoughts, even more perhaps, than our academic education; at least for a while.
To such an extent, in fact, that we at the Nook form a band...
We like to call it a band – in fact we call it 'The Nook Band,' as its members live in the house, but it's not what others might call a band. Certainly not at the beginning! We *do* have three guitarists. Two of whom are actually very good. The third is learning to play: he can manage about three chords. A couple of people sing, one bashes tambourine, and I have a pair of inverted plastic buckets, which I deludedly believe I can play like Santana's Michael Shrieve.
We are catastrophically bad.
Against all the odds, some people like us (or maybe pity us) enough for us to get gigs. Yes, gigs! People even applaud!
At the beginning, these are exclusively in the student's union folk club, a small but nonetheless popular and modestly prestigious venue. We learn new songs. We harmonise. We improve, and eventually we even get to play at bigger events,

History of a Daft A'porth

such as those that take place in the students' union refectory, with *proper* bands. We have a starry future ahead of us...
And then the live-in girlfriend of one guitarist falls in love with the other guitarist, with predictable consequences.
The Nook Band is no more.
Some of us carry on singing or playing as 'independent artists' (local folk clubs, open mic nights etc), but the band never reforms. My hopes of eclipsing Ginger Baker are cruelly dashed.

Drugs...

I'm in bed on a Sunday morning when the doorbell rings. It's 8.15, and I'm still a bit pissed from the party last night. Who would be calling on us at this hour – especially on a Sunday? I glance across at Keith in his pit on the other side of the room. No movement; so I get up, exit our ground floor room, and open the front door. There are two men in suits outside.
"Morning sir, I'm sergeant __, and this is constable __. I believe you had a party here last night?" He shows me his badge.
I'm frozen with fear, but manage, "Yes."
We did have a party here last night, a loud music, drunken, shouty, comings-and-goings, spilling-on-to-the-street, annoy-our-remarkably-tolerant-under-the-circumstances-neighbours kind of party. A copious amount of marijuana was consumed in many and various forms. Mostly it was smoked in joints, the remnants of which are all over the house. Roaches: bits of rolled up cardboard in cigarette papers – the 'filter tip' of the pot-head – lie in heaps in ashtrays. The house reeks of dope.
And now there are two policemen at the door...
"Er, what's it about?"
"Did you know everyone there, sir?"
"Er, no, there were loads... we never know everyone...I don't..."
I trail off, mouth flapping like a cod in a boat.
"Well there was a bit of trouble, sir. An elderly lady around the back there," – he nods at 'round the back' – "had some bottles thrown through her window, and they can only have been thrown from your garden."

"Oh my god... that's awful... that's really terrible...I...er..."
I trail away, flapping again (Haddock, this time?). But thank God: they're not here about the dope!

"Can we come in and talk about it sir?"

"Of course." I step back.

But where to? The living room is an Aladdin's cave of joint residue, so in desperation I lead them back into our bedroom, hoping it's escaped amassing anything obvious during the party.

The sergeant positions himself comfortably in the middle of the room, while the constable rests his arm on top of my big chest of drawers. About ten centimeters from his elbow, inside the top drawer, is a lump of cannabis resin the size of a stock cube. I try not to stare so hard at the drawer that he'll be irresistibly drawn to open it.

The sergeant and I proceed to have a terribly serious conversation about the thoughtless idiots who have terrified this poor old lady beyond our back garden, smashing her window with thrown bottles in the middle of the night. (Why didn't the police come at the time? I silently wonder), and how I too am outraged, and will go round myself to fix her window and clear up all the mess, and I am so, so, sorry that she has been put through this, and of course we'll make sure this never happens again at any of our parties, and... "This time," he interjects, "as you're being so helpful, Sir, and you're obviously very upset by it, we won't take it any further," and he'll be checking to make sure I do what I have said, and "Thank you very much sir." I glance across at Keith, whose duvet is pulled up to his nose, revealing only his wide-open eyes.

I see the two men out; they quite amicably say their goodbyes, and I stumble back into our room.

If they'd gone into the living room! Couldn't they smell it? What if they'd looked in the drawer?

But they didn't; we're unscathed.

I look over again at Keith. His eyes are still visible above the Duvet, like a magician's rabbit who's mis-timed his appearance. He blinks, and sits up, and we stare silently at each other for what seems like hours. Then we laugh like drains with relief.

History of a Daft A'porth

Later, Keith will swear blind he slept through the whole episode. This is my first brush with the law since that day when I fled the carving knife as a child, and it has left me both relieved and stunned. That afternoon, I keep my word, and go round to clear up and replace the broken glass, and to apologise. It's a salutary lesson on what alcohol will do to one's hold on sensible behaviour. Unfortunately, that's a lesson it will take me personally many more years to really learn.

At school, no-one smoked pot, as we called it then. The drug of choice was Players No 10, a small, cheap, nasty brand of cigarettes, which were mostly consumed in the traditional haunts of the bogs and the bike sheds. I didn't smoke then, and the smell of stale cigarettes and urine repelled me sufficiently to keep it that way while I was at school.
At university in 1969, however, it's cool to smoke, and not long after freshers' week, I succumb to the offer of one. It's not the first time I've ever tried, but the result is predictable... a fair amount of coughing and lightheadedness, but I persevere. I will – thank goodness – never be a heavy smoker. I become what's laughingly called a social smoker. In other words, only when I'm having a drink, or on the odd occasion when I want to look extra cool! (The next year, on holiday in France, I smoke Gitanes, on the beach... they are absolutely vile, but oh la la, très chic!)
Inevitably, given the student monoculture of the early 1970's, I join the dope-smoking fraternity – which is, frankly, almost everybody. It's mostly at parties. I don't walk around with a joint dangling from my lips – at least not often, but I begin to buy my own, and discover the delights of grass, feeling quite Californian as I enjoy the crack and spit of seeds in our smouldering joints.
Booze is as much a part of student life as dope, and it too is consumed in vast quantities. In freshers' week, I go on the pub marathon. We run ten pubs on a circuit of the town, knocking back a very swift half pint in each. I make it to the eighth before throwing up, but finish the course. As distinct from smoking, I've had an intensive apprenticeship with booze in my teens, and have gained my stripes!

Despite all this, I consider myself a moderate drinker and smoker. Some of my friends consume enormous amounts of one or the other, or both; some with sad consequences. Abstemious only by comparison, I avoid the worst.

Nonetheless, during my time at university there are many, many events that take place under one kind of influence or another; some of which are funny, some not, and some of which will resurface in my memory over the years, with various levels of embarrassment or amusement.

Viz:

Coming home at two a.m. from a party, very, very drunk, I collapse on the pavement, and flailing like an upturned beetle, can't persuade my legs to stand me up for several minutes. During this, at least one other person staggers past without offering to help, or even seeming to notice me, and carries on their way.

At one of the Nook parties, after several joints, I find myself helpless with giggles at the bottom of the stairs on my knees, unable to make it any further up. I can't stop laughing, and finally giving up the attempt to climb, I crawl back into the living room, where my mates and I continue to giggle for an indefinite period till we simultaneously get the munchies, and disperse – still giggling – to unearth something to eat.

My friend Dave has had way too much to drink in a local pub. Suddenly, the booze gets the better of his stomach, and he feels it rise. Dave's a considerate chap. He's sat opposite me between two other mates, and puts his hand in front of his mouth to save me from the projectile vomiting he knows is imminent. Sadly, this has the effect of rerouting a considerable quantity of it to each side, drenching both his neighbours in a vigorous, Monty-Python-like stream of fluid. Once again, I suffer aching ribs from an extended, alcohol-fueled bout of helpless laughter as my mates drip sick, and Dave mumbles dribbling, abject apologies.

History of a Daft A'porth

A student house party – one of many – is untypically flaccid. Bored, I leave. On my way out, I spot two unopened seven–pint cans (very popular at this time), which I 'liberate.' I've come on my five hundred cc BSA, a brute of a bike that sounds like an angry farm tractor. Mounting it, and having no other means of portage, I somehow wedge a can between each elbow and thigh, and set off. It's around one a.m., there's hardly any traffic, and I have an uninterrupted journey home. Almost...

There're lights halfway down the steep hill from which two swift left turns will bring me to the Nook. Up till now, I haven't had to stop, but the lights are red. Despite my rebel principles and my anti-establishment politics, I'm quite well behaved, and red means stop – empty road, deserted streets or not. I decelerate as gently as possible. "Go green, go green!" But no. At this time of night, traffic light timings are longer. Red persists, and I come to a gradual, dead halt. The bike is big. Heavy. Lots of inertia. It doesn't want to tip. But, inevitably, it starts. I have a choice now: put my foot down to stabilize the bike, thus dropping a can, or hang on to both cans in the desperate hope the lights will change just in time. It's a juvenile dilemma. By the time I decide, it's too late, the bike has reached the point of no return, and has tipped beyond my ability to support it. Over we go. The cans fall, and one of them sets off rolling down the hill. The heavy BSA has fallen with the foot-rest between my foot and the sole of my boot – effectively pinning me beneath the machine like a cowboy under a dead horse. Although unhurt, I can't move. I'm trapped. I could be here till morning...

At this moment I see cresting the rise on the opposite side of the road, a middle-aged couple, presumably returning from their own night out. He in flat cap and Donkey-jacket, she in headscarf and big woolen coat. They spot me, and there is a moment. Then they rush across, "Y'oright son?" (broad Sheffield). He grabs the bike, and with enormous effort begins to lift. As we crank me slowly upright, I watch his wife – of maybe sixty – turn, hoik up her skirt, take a breath, and begin a vigorous pursuit of the can that is now accelerating merrily downhill away from the lights (currently green, of course). And she catches it. Returning, beaming in triumph and breathing heavily, she plonks it down on the pavement with the other one, and says, "There y' go luv. Couldn't let 'im get away, could we?" They brush me down, ensure I'm unharmed, say a breezy farewell, and disappear into the night. I drive the remaining fifty meters home, park the bike, and return on foot to recoup my beer. The lights turn red again as I walk away.

There are many, many such occurrences, the less lighthearted of which might easily result in serious hurt or even death, but my friends and I get away with it, and never cause or suffer injury. And although many around me are doing it, I never drop acid. I have heard too many descriptions of bad trips, and on balance, I'm not willing to risk it. A friend of mine gives me a line of coke to try. It does absolutely nothing for me, and I have to conclude that, either coke has no effect on me, or it was baking powder. Either way, I never bother again, and the idea of heroin frankly scares the crap out of me.

Over the years, the excesses subside. I adopt a more moderate consumption of alcohol, and later, will hardly ever smoke a joint, only rarely indulging in the latter when offered at a party or by a house guest. Eventually, along with cigarettes, I'll give it up altogether. I can't say the same for alcohol, which will remain a moderate, if constant and pleasurable vice.

Sex...
Ahh.... The swinging sixties...
In fact, I've been at school for most of them; I arrive at university in 1969, and the whole apparent point of the swinging sixties appears to have passed me by completely. I'm still a virgin, dammit! I have of course very much discovered girls, and I find them mightily attractive, but my brief 'relationships' so far have served simply to feed a growing lack of self confidence in that department. I've been dumped and/or stood-up by pretty much all of the girls who've consented to go out with me, and ignored or snubbed by many other objects of my longing. I know

History of a Daft A'porth

that I should just 'let it happen,' and not try too hard. Yet all around me at university are couples, obviously having sex – not publicly, of course, although some will do just that occasionally – and a few of whom are apparently in love. I don't really know what I most feel the lack of, sex or love? Is it both? This is the era of 'Free Love,' whatever that actually means. It certainly does *not* mean that any girl you fancy will jump into bed with you. Quite right too of course, but as is probably evident, I've not yet fully unpacked feminism. Although I generously regard girls as being equal to boys in many ways, I've a fair way to go in that direction as yet.

Luckily, in this liberated and politically progressive climate, as in most student bodies of this period, the prejudices and half-formed social mores with which I left school have come under immediate and sustained attack. I'm beginning to properly understand such ideas as class structure, social mobility, equal rights, women's liberation, etc, and to align myself with the struggles against racism, sexism, homophobia, and 'the man.' This last is somewhat hypocritical on all our parts, as it's 'the man' who provides our grants, teaches us, maintains the roads, and keeps us safe and healthy. But we are a new wave. We protest; we sit in; we march. Gradually we evolve, we *do* become more aware, even a bit more *self*-ware. We see that band of Hamburg fame with the Maharishi, we collect money for the striking miners, we abhor the political right, we witness in privileged horror the savagery of the Vietnam war. It doesn't take long to grow up a tad in this kind of environment. Whether it's the changes that all of this engenders in me, or simply that I'll stop trying too hard to 'have a girlfriend,' or something else entirely...? I won't ever really know. But eventually, even this will resolve.

It does. The great *event* happens. Unfortunately, for me, as it is for many – boys *and* girls – losing my virginity is not the joyful event it's cracked up to be.

I get fairly drunk at a party, and find myself chatting with an equally drunken girl. We end up eating each other's faces on a couch somewhere, and she comes back to the Nook with me. We have drunkenly unsatisfactory sex. In the morning we both endure an excruciating hour or so as we get up, have coffee, and I walk her home, both of us in the full knowledge that I'm not in the slightest bit interested in continuing the relationship. She's not *the one*. This is *not* the love-filled flowering of adulthood I was expecting, and neither, I'm convinced, is it hers. I shall forever hold onto the shame of this moment. Although yes, we were *both* consenting adults, I treat her gracelessly, and with little respect. It's not supposed to be like this; I feel horribly guilty, and I become lonelier and more depressed. I fervently hope my 'first one' will go on to find someone who will treat her better than I.

It'll be months before I discover how wonderful the real thing can be.

The real thing turns out to be Alison, a first year (I'm now in my second) from Cheshire. I'm happily stunned when she agrees to my invitation to go see a band, and even more stunned when she appears to be as interested in me as I am in her. She's beautiful, sexy, smart, funny, and apparently finds me attractive. Whoopee!

We have sex at every possible opportunity. She lives in a hall of residence, and I spend practically every night there – when she's not at the Nook. We visit her parents during the Easter holiday, and have sex on the living room floor after they've gone to bed. In the local park, we secrete ourselves deep in the bushes, and have sex. We do other things apart from have sex of course, and it's all wonderful. I'm in love. This is the real thing. The long vacation arrives, and she returns home for the summer. No text or email in these times, and as we're both busy, we don't write or call. I eagerly await her return.

Summer ends, and Alison returns for the start of a new term. I'm so pleased she's back, I'm almost tearful.

Then I see the look on her face. It's that mixture of guilt, sadness, and defiance we wear when about to say something we know will hurt. I brace myself.

History of a Daft A'porth

"I'm sorry Pete, I can't be with you anymore"
"What do you mean?"
"It's just... not right... You're not right for me."
"Why? what have I done?"
"Nothing, I... Nothing. You just... I just ... I just can't anymore."
Then that awful phrase...
"It's not you, it's me."
It will be a while, but I'll only really understand what that phrase means when I dig it out to say to someone else.
I'm dumped, and I'm wretched. I plead, I beg, I weep. She's obdurate. But she says she still "cares a lot for me, so let's go to bed for a last time". I'll look back on this with mixed feelings. Yes, it was a genuine act of pity and affection on her part. Yes, I desperately wanted it. Should I have agreed? Did it change anything for better or worse? I will never be sure. We do go to bed, and the sex is tender, but tearful. Afterwards, she kisses me goodbye, and leaves forever. I weep again. The end of the affair.
I'm desolated by Alison's departure. The collapse of my first love affair leaves me vulnerable and probably a bit desperate. I'm discovering that I'm not truly happy unless I'm with someone, and I spend the next few years in and out of short-term or very short-term relationships with girls who 'do not live up to my idea of the perfect one;' some of whom break my heart, and some of whose hearts I break with my own abrupt ending of the affair. This is by either moving callously on to someone new who has 'stolen me away;' or, like Alison, simply being unable to continue with something false. I'm still consciously or unconsciously, looking for 'the one.' I begin to wonder if such a person exists, or whether she's simply a construct I've swallowed whole from works of fiction.

There are many theories about romantic love. Aristophanes suggests that humans were originally one organism with two faces, four arms, four legs etc, and that they were split apart by the gods, to spend their lives searching for their literal other halves; Freud posits, among other things, that we base our adult relationships on those of our parents (Not me!); Sternberg proposes that love is a triangular interaction between intimacy, passion, and commitment; and in 1974, American psychologist Zick Rubin even develops a scale to measure these elements. However we may regard these various theories about love, most of us seem to recognise it when we see it, and to know when we feel it.

If reciprocated, it's euphoric, uplifting, joyful, and fulfilling; if unrequited, it can be crushing, tearful, lonely, and bitter. It can surreptitiously creep up and invade you, or it can hit you like the proverbial express train. Of all the emotions, love is arguably the most varied in its manifestations. It can lead to extraordinary acts of kindness, generosity, and sacrifice, or it can cause people to commit murder or suicide. It can transform itself into the other emotions – joy, ecstasy, sadness, despair, anger, fear, hate. It inspires great works of art and literature: it starts wars. Some live their whole lives without it; a few are lucky enough to be enfolded in it from cradle to grave. Most of us, of course, are at some point along that line between the two extremes, and most of us experience at least some of the happiness and the sadness it can bring – many of us, more than once. If we take notice of what our friends say, of what is in the media, and of what appears in small ads (which will at some distant time in the future become dating apps), most of us are constantly in search of it.

I'm no different. And alone, I'm as mournful and bereft as Elvis's hound dog.

Then in 1975 I meet Viv.

I'm directing a revue for Rag committee in freshers' week. This happens every year as one of the events raising money for charities supported by the students' union. Usually, these revues are utter rubbish; badly written, disorganized, and poorly performed. This year, Rag Committee have asked Theatre Group to take it over, and it's fallen to me. Apparently, by dint of hard work, I've gained some reputation for knowing – as well as any – what I'm doing.

I trawl various sources for decent material (including the union toilets, every square inch of which is covered with incredibly

History of a Daft A'porth

creative and scurrilously funny graffiti), I write a framework script to be workshopped, with songs, and I audition and cast half a dozen actors from theatre group, some of whom will become close friends.

One of these is Viv.

She's petite, very sharp, very funny, very pretty, and lives up to her name – vivacious. I'm instantly smitten. But we have a job to do, and I mustn't let my feelings get in the way. I have a point to prove: that this show can be done properly. So we improvise, rehearse, rewrite, rehearse more, and bit by bit it all takes respectable shape. As things progress, I think I sense a reciprocal attraction from Viv, and I have to find out if I'm right. The traditional two performances of the revue are a resounding success. People who have seen previous ones tell us they 'never knew it could be a proper show.' We're exalted, and at the end of the second evening we're all invited by Viv for celebratory drinks to her hall of residence room. Everyone's on top of the world, and we gabble on for hours about how brilliant and wonderful we all are. It gets very late. A few of us are sat on the bed, and I lie back yawning, sleepily closing my eyes. The rest of the group carry on talking for what seems like forever, until someone finally suggests it's time to go. I'm hoping they'll think I'm conked out. Either I'll be woken and taken away, or (I plead with the universe) Viv will suggest they leave me be, and she'll wake me later when I've had some of the sleep I obviously need as their exhausted director...

"It's OK, I'll deal with him... don't wake him up, he's knackered," she says.

I give silent thanks, just managing to not react, and continue to 'sleep'. Everyone knows what's going on, but plays the game. Farewell hugs are exchanged, and the others leave. Viv lets me lie a little while she tidies up, and then she wakes me. I feign doziness, and apologise, but she gently shushes me with a finger on my lips, leans in, and kisses me with blissful tenderness.

I don't go home that night.

It's the beginning of something amazing. That missing half for which I've been searching for so long. Whatever it is, she has it in spades. That spark between us, that Aristophanian connection.

We will be together for five years; the longest intimate relationship I've had up to now lasted less than a year. Making the most of the liberal moral climate in seventies student Britain, we explore our sexuality, experimenting with other partners – a threesome or two, and so-on. We try a so-called open relationship, but despite the claims circulating in the new moral universe, that new relationship formats are part of the sexual revolution, and that old norms are disappearing, this experiment eventually succumbs to the demands of conventional couple fidelity. Conventional or not, during our five years together, our lives will be filled with events both joyful and tragic. We move in together; we split up and reunite; we play William Blake and wife Kate in Adrian Mitchel's *Tyger*; we swelter through the great drought of 1976; support each other through the tragedy of a friend's suicide; have fights; make up; start new careers, and change each other's lives. For a while, it seems as though it will never end.

But it does.

Viv abandons university for a speech therapy course in Leicester, and for various reasons, I have to seek work in London. The cracks begin to show.

It's hard keeping a long-distance relationship going. I'm sternly reminded by our friends that it takes work and commitment. Unfortunately, neither of us appear willing to undertake either of these in the required amount. It seems we're not the perfect other halves we first thought.

We still feel deeply for each other, though, and when we finally split up, it is like the end of a marriage; I for one, am heartbroken. Now living in different cities, we don't even get to say goodbye face to face. We'll never see or hear from each other again. It's the close of a chapter.

These loves, these pivotal people; these formative years in Sheffield; student life, friends, first romance, music, politics, new beginnings in new places... all these influences, have made a

History of a Daft A'porth

start – a very tentative start – on a long process: that of taking the wet-behind-the-ears adolescent sporting blazer and slacks, fresh from school in 1969 with his juvenile prejudices and half-formed ideas... and moulding him into some semblance of an adult being... dare I say... a man?

Sex 'n Drugs 'n Rock and Roll truly are, as Ian Dury says, "very good indeed."

But let's not forget that at university one is also supposed to get a more obvious kind of education.

Peter Benson

Chapter 8: Academia

The University brings out all abilities, including incapability.
    Anton Chekhov

As they say in the movies... *Six years earlier...*

"You should apply for Cambridge."
Our school careers master. Or the nearest thing to it. I.e. the teacher who has had the post foisted on him. "And you should apply for economics... And accountancy. You're a bright lad. They're great careers. Or law?"
I have *no* idea. I'm sixteen, for goodness' sake; how the hell do *I* know what I want to do? I accept the proposed choices with the gratitude of the desperate.
As prompted, I apply to Cambridge, along with the five other universities I'm entitled to under UCCA rules: Sheffield, Hull, Nottingham, Southampton, and Aston.
I get interviews at most of them, including Cambridge, and for the thrill of the journey, I go to every one. I've not travelled so much on my own since the Air Cadets.
All the universities are interesting solely because I've never seen one before. The redbrick ones are monstrous, unattractive blocks, faceless, and slightly intimidating, in uncompromising, hard-edged, high-rise cityscapes or isolated, modernist campuses. Cambridge is different: similarly intimidating, but also beautiful and serene. I'm enchanted by the fairy-tale quality of buildings and setting; students out on the lawns or punting down the river, gothic college quads, and medieval-fronted bookshops; It's cinematically romantic.
My interview is at once otherworldly and unnerving. The interviewer is such an amalgam of erudite, obscure, and avuncular, that I find it impossible to figure out whether he is encouraging or mocking, and I'm left unsure whether or not I've made a complete fool of myself. It's a surreal experience.
Despite this, they offer me two A's and a B. Not bad, considering.

History of a Daft A'porth

Not bad, but I don't get it. I get A, B, and two D's.

I rationalise magnificently, deciding I never really wanted to go to Cambridge – toffee-nosed, elitist, ritual-engorged theme park that it obviously is...!

My second choice, Sheffield (my first, really), offered me ADD, so I'm in!

I'm going with my school's recommendations of Economics and Accountancy. Sheffield, however, requires a tripartite first year; I have to pick a third subject. My 'A' at A-level was in General Studies, a subject often regarded by those not taking it as a bit of a doddle. In fact, it was anything but, and because of its scope and the tutorial-like way it was taught, it probably did more than most other subjects to encourage independent and original thinking in those taking it. Part of the course was an introduction to psychology, and I loved it. I found it novel, fascinating and instructive. Consequently, psychology is the course I now choose to complete my tripartite first year at Sheffield.

Follows, the whirlwind of registration and freshers' week; settling into accommodation; making friends, and exploring the university and town.

Courses start.

Over the next few weeks, three things become clear.

First, I really enjoy psychology. It continues to engage and illuminate.

Secondly, Economics, though not difficult, bores the pants off me.

Thirdly, and worryingly, I'm completely baffled by the legal, logistical, and regulatory complexities of accountancy. I'm being left behind!

Something's very wrong; if I want to be here next year, I have to remedy it, and soon.

I'm not too worried about passing psychology. My tutor is very encouraging, and I don't find the research or the essays daunting. I'm pretty sure I'll manage the end-of-year exams.

It also becomes rapidly evident that my economics lectures are simply a verbal iteration of the main text book – Lipsey. I buy a second-hand copy, read it several times over the year, attend tutorials, write the required essays, and never go to another economics lecture.

Accountancy is the big problem, so I approach my tutor. This kind and perceptive man is a lesson in all a tutor should be. He rapidly assesses that I'm a classic square peg in a round hole, and proposes a system of extra help and revision. All being well, this will provide me the necessary minimum knowledge to scale the wall that is first year exams.

With the support of this shrewd and generous tutor, text-book Lipsey, and, it has to be said, with a good deal of slog from me, I make it to the end of my first year.

I pass the exams in all three subjects. Phew!

What now? I could go on and do psychology to degree level, surely? But somehow, it doesn't feel right. Of the three subjects available to me, two were thrust upon me by my school. I don't really have a choice of three, I have a choice of one. I'm youthfully arrogant and indignant enough to feel this is unacceptable, and something should be done about it. (A petulant stamp of the foot would be appropriate here).

I get an appointment to see the dean of the faculty of social sciences, and explain my predicament. I make the case that I've been deprived of a relevant choice of subjects in my first year, and as such there are none with which I can reasonably compare psychology. The whole point of the tripartite first year – as stated in Sheffield's prospectus, I loftily point out, is to encourage a balanced and rational choice at the end of it. For me, this is impossible, as economics and accountancy are totally inappropriate subjects, and I have thus, effectively, only one option.

This cannot be just, I insist, and I propose a retake of the first year with subjects of my choosing – arrived at from a much more informed position, thus enabling me to make a pedagogically valid decision at the end of the year.

To my utter astonishment, he's in complete agreement.

History of a Daft A'porth

I can take another first year doing my own subject selection of Politics, Sociology, and Philosophy. As long as I get a grant for the extra year from the Local Education Authority (LEA) in Halifax.

This is long before student loans. We baby boomers have the extraordinarily good fortune to live in a time when all our tuition fees are paid. In addition, based on parental income, you're given a maintenance grant. This to be topped up if necessary by your family. If your parental income is low enough, you're awarded a 'full grant.' Effectively, this is enough to house you, feed you, buy your books, etc, and even offer the possibility of some entertainment, for the whole of your university career. What differs radically from the system that from 1990 will begin to replace the current one, and in doing so divide the nation, is that we do *not* have to pay it back. Ever. Looking back, much later, whilst watching our children painfully shoulder the burden of student loans, we'll realise how very lucky we were, and how onerous the system will become.

It's *just* enough, but it is enough. And because my family's dirt poor, I'm entitled to the full amount.

So, at the end of term, I go back to Halifax, and I apply for the extra year's grant.

I receive a reply, generously offering the cash when the LEA have received proof of my acceptance onto the course.

I write to the faculty, explaining the request, and they reply that they're happy to admit me to the course when they have confirmation that I'll receive the relevant financial support from the LEA.

Mmmm...

Back to the LEA. "Sorry, we can't give you a grant until you've been accepted on a course. That's the regulation."

Back to Sheffield. "Sorry, we can't accept you on the course until you've been given a grant. That's the regulation."

We go back and forth several times until it becomes evident that this impasse is set in steel-reinforced bureaucratic concrete.

It looks as if I must either give in, and just move on – miffed or not – to second year psychology, or give up university altogether.

Stubbornly unwilling to do either of these, I rack my brains for another option, and come up with a plan. Of sorts. With my admittedly feeble grasp of accounting, I decide that if I can get a job over the summer, then along with part-time work in term-time, I could support myself through the next academic year. I'm far too proud and obstinate to accept the other alternatives.

There's a new building site not far from the Nook. McAlpine's are putting up a building supplies warehouse. I apply for a job. They're short-handed (thank you, 1970s full employment), and the next week I abruptly find myself wheeling barrowloads of wet mortar up and down the site to supply the bricklayers. It's awful, backbreaking work. The full barrows are only just within my capacity to lift, and particularly difficult and precarious to push up the inevitable steep and bouncy planks; the handles are covered with wet cement, and rub my hands raw, and the sloppy contents constantly threaten to upend themselves in a watery grey lava-flow that muggins will have to clear up; it's exhausting, repetitive and boring, and I snootily despair of my work companions' endless discussions of football and Page 3 pin-ups. As the weeks progress, at least I develop some muscles, and the barrowloads become consequently easier, but I'm not sure I'll be able to stand this over the long term.

Then I have another of my bright ideas.

I approach the site manager, and ask for a word. He's going to be running the place when it's finished. Busy though he is, he's seen that I work hard, and grants audience. In his office I put it to him that, having eight O-levels, and 4 A-levels, I can surely be of more use to him than wheeling wet sludge around all day.

There's a skeptical pause, then once again to my astonishment, agreement.

"Take this clipboard and these notes, and start checking the supplies in the new timber storage shed. You can run that when it's finished... if you think you're up to it."

"Absolutely!" (It can't be rocket science can it?)

History of a Daft A'porth

"You can start now. Off you go then."

Wow... suddenly, I'm management.

So off I go, clipboard in hand... My erstwhile colleagues regard me with new-found respect. (Ha! Ha!).

A week later a letter arrives from the dean of social sciences; he can see the idiocy of the Kafkaesque bureaucracy preventing me from fulfilling my destiny, and has cut the red tape with a big pair of scissors. He's written to the LEA to tell them I've been accepted onto the course. Three days later, the LEA writes to me to say I *will* receive the extra grant. I whoop with joy, relief, and eternal gratitude to my saviour the dean of Social Sciences for his clear-sighted pragmatism and decisive action.

The following day, with fulsome thanks for his faith in me, I hand in my week's notice to the site manager. He is *not* pleased, and I'm asked to leave with immediate effect. Let's hope I never need a job there again! I think my arms must be an inch longer thanks to the cement-laden wheelbarrows, but when I return to Alice's for the remainder of the holiday, and apply for the bins again, I find I can throw them around with the best of them. I do this for a couple of weeks, have a bit of a break, and then it's back to Sheffield for what I consider to be my *real* first year; Politics, Sociology, and Philosophy.

This is more like it! I'm settled in as a second-year veteran, and so have a certain caché with the other, younger members of my courses, (At least for the first few weeks!) I know my way around a textbook, have mastered the intricacies of the library, and my social life is established. This is how my *first* first-year should have gone, but I don't regret the hiccup that led me to this point. I learned a lot from it, particularly about not taking things for granted – my entitlement to education, as a prime example: only five percent of schoolchildren go on to university in the sixties. It's the start of a realization that I'm now part of a rather privileged minority. The content of the courses I'm now doing also contributes to this growing enlightenment. Every student should have a healthy dose of sociology and politics thrown at them for their own good! As Andy Hargreaves and many other commentators will point out, we're part of an almost unique cohort. We will benefit from the social mobility provided by an education policy that's enlightened and forward-thinking, but tragically short-lived. This policy has allowed me and my peers to make it to university despite formidable barriers of poverty and class, and I've carried here with me an acute sensibility of my difficult childhood. This, along with a growing socio-political awareness, has led to a sense of differing from many of my fellow students, and to a sizeable chip on my shoulder. Most of my friends here are from solidly middle-class backgrounds, one or two are even landed gentry! They've benefitted from supportive families and all the advantages of healthy incomes, travel, tutors, coaches etc. Many of my working-class peers and I, on the other hand, 'have got here solely on merit and grit,' and when it comes to academic achievement, we're a match for them. It'll be a while before we acknowledge our massive and distorted resentment, and exchange it for a more rational and dispassionate analysis. But we can still drink them all under the table.

(Well, some of them!)

The year goes by. I am perfectly at home in all three of my second-first-year subjects; I find them equally stimulating and absorbing. Because of this, my extra year, and the increased confidence and experience it's given me, I have no great difficulty passing the end-of-year exams... for the second time!

Housemate Bob and I go hitch hiking around Europe for a month. I take a holiday job during the remaining weeks of the vacation, and at the start of the next term, I must decide which of the now *four* viable subjects I shall be pursuing to degree level.

Despite the kerfuffle, and notwithstanding the interest I've found in the other disciplines, I decide to continue with psychology. At the start of all this I'd 'warned' the Faculty that I might, but no-one seems in the least bothered. So little fuss is made, in fact, that I'm given to wonder if this changing horses isn't unusual. Given the state of career advice – certainly at my school – I wouldn't be surprised.

My third year.

History of a Daft A'porth

Life in the psychology department is a mix of weird experiments, boring statistics, and fascinating insights into human and animal behaviour, and I enjoy my next two years. The students' union activities, sport, and my friends, offer a huge number of attractive diversions, however, and as a result my academic achievements are never outstanding. But I do throw myself into it, and the grounding I had in the sixth form proves itself at least a bit useful. The course includes: illuminating revelations about why we do what we do and think as we think; detailed study of the brain and the nervous system, with its various receptor and motor interactions; and tedious, but necessarily complex statistics required for experimental data analysis.

Some of the coursework we study is revelatory: The Stanford Prison Guard experiments reveal we all have the capacity to be corrupted by power; the subjects in the Milgram study of obedience to authority agree to administer what they believed were electric shocks well beyond the pain threshold; Bowlby's experiments on monkeys throw light on maternal deprivation and attachment disorders; and many, many others illustrate how extremely fallible we humans are.

Other examples are more optimistic. One American study shows how we react positively to touch. Experimenters had asked unsuspecting subjects if they had found a coin left behind in a phone box they had just used. Those who were lightly touched when asked were far more likely to hand over the coin they had just pocketed.

We also get to be experimental subjects. We long to be part of some ground-breaking, world-changing study, but sadly, most of the tasks we're asked to perform are pedestrian exercises in visual recognition, optical illusion, or other aspects of sensory perception, a field in which the Psychology department at Sheffield specialises. We spend a lot of time pressing buttons in response to flashing lights or buzzers and bells. It's all a bit like an extended vision and hearing test at Boots!

In a tip of the hat to the climate of 'counter-culture' that's swirling around in the UK, Europe, and America, we also cast an eye on the less orthodox practitioners waving their pennants on the field of academic battle. We're introduced (albeit with a slightly disapproving air) to such luminaries of the unconventional approach as RD Laing and Timothy Leary – both proponents of non-interventionist psychiatry and the use of LSD as a therapeutic drug. They claim it's better to allow those classed as mentally ill to work their own way through their issues, and that their states of mind are simply "differences" and not "illnesses." This is directly connected to the ideas of ancient (and some contemporary) peoples to whom the status of such individuals is special: shaman or priest. It's intriguing, although not strictly within the course's remit (psychiatry being a branch of medicine, and therefore separate from psychology for our purposes). Paradoxically, reading them only confirms my decision not to take acid, but it does open up a new strand of reading. Through Kerouac's *On the Road*, Huxley's *The Doors of Perception*, and others of that ilk, my view of the mind and the self perversely becomes even less sure than it previously was. I used to have a reasonable sense of the distinction between the two, but three years of a psychology degree, my expanding literary horizons, and regular blows to many of the certainties of life, have rather diluted that. Nevertheless, psychology proves a good choice for me. It's an absorbing discipline. At once academic and practical, it seems to attract interesting people, and, yes, it does help one to understand oneself a little better. Just a little. This is something many of us long for; I do, certainly. It goes part way to explaining why people behave the way they do. There's a downside, however. We psychology students suffer almost universally from an inflated sense of self-worth because we're convinced we 'know how people tick.' We also know, but rarely admit, that this is egotistical, hugely generalized, and in truth, an arrogance. Deep down, though, we can't rid ourselves of the delusion that we have just a teensy bit of superior knowledge. On revealing what subject, we do, we frequently get the response, "Well what am I thinking now then?" We usually reply either with a flippant "Look into my eyes...!" (especially if we're flirting), or by launching into a long and lofty explanation of the difference between mind-reading

History of a Daft A'porth

and the serious scientific study of behaviour, followed by the consequences of this, both good and bad, for humanity. We alone can save the world! As our studies progress, however, we begin to grasp more and more how psychology is used and abused, consciously or unconsciously, in almost every aspect of life (as evidenced in the above experiments). As with any field of study, psychology, and the insights gained from it, are tools which in the wrong hands can be weaponized. Any mechanism that allows us to manipulate human behaviour, from whatever discipline the knowledge is gleaned, must be recognized as the double-edged sword it is, and cautiously and respectfully handled, or there will be trouble!

Being a psychology student has perks. As well as the (tiny) fees we're offered as experimental subjects, I get to earn a few quid on a regular basis by spending long hours of my spare time transcribing data onto punch cards for the department's computer. Before the days of miniaturization take off, this machine fills an entire room, uses thousands of punch cards, and reels and reels of one-inch magnetic tape. I spend endless hours mindlessly typing at one of the three heavy-keyed terminals, entering scores from questionnaires filled out by experimental subjects. It occurs to me in passing, that, ironically, I must at some point have anonymously entered several of my own test scores.

I've also become a regular member of the psychology department cricket team.

I had hoped to represent the university on the sports field, so I tried out for the rugby team. But I found the style of play too aggressive – not at all the relatively gentlemanly game I was used to at school. Hence my 'defection' to the departmental cricket squad. I've even distinguished myself with some spectacular diving catches, though I do not go on to greater things.

During the long summer vacations, when I'm not punching in test scores, I go back to Halifax and work variously on the dustbins, at Crossley's Carpets driving a fork lift truck (some of the best fun I will ever have in a workplace), and later, at Bachelors' Foods in Sheffield. What most occupies my mind during the vacation following my second year of psychology, is what on earth am I going to do for my final year's dissertation? Despite my interest in the subject, I've no idea what field to choose, and even less in which topic to specialize in for the study.

A close friend of mine is vice chairman of Student Reception, a student-run organisation jointly funded by the university and the students' union. SR is responsible for meeting, greeting, and showing around sixth formers up for interview. We arrange accommodation, should they need it, and give them a little chat about what life is *really* like at university – as opposed to what they read in prospectuses: study, health, finance, entertainment, lodging, personal issues, etc. We also set up and successfully run a one-day conference for local schools, which goes down so well, the following year we create a three-day one with national catchment. As an organisation, SR becomes so successful that other universities set up copycat bodies.

All this wins us lots of brownie points from the university, but takes up rather a large amount of our time. I become Vice President of the society, and thus even more involved. Probably because of this, allied to an inability to decide on anything else, I choose for my dissertation a study of the influence of photography in prospectuses on the choice of university made by candidates: i.e. If there are more and better photos in its brochure, is that institution more likely to be higher in the applicant's list of choices? My tutor is dubious at first, but we go ahead; I carry out an in-depth statistical study based on as many prospectuses I can amass, plus data on their selections from a sufficiently large cohort of candidates. When I look back at the ridiculously lightweight nature of this study, I'm astounded that I found twenty thousand words to write on it. Nonetheless, at the end of my course I'm smugly delighted to have proven – with high statistical significance – that the greater use of photography *does* have an effect on university choice. World changing stuff... it gets me a 2.2. Ah, well...

Oh, and I forgot to mention: at the beginning of my second year at university, I acquired what every footloose student needs... a dog!

Chapter 9: Frodo

If I could be half the person my dog is, I'd be twice the human I am.
Charles Yu

"A dog! You've got to be crazy!" My house mate, Bob when I arrive back after the summer break with said dog in tow. He may be right. Why did I get a dog? I don't really know. A few weeks ago, I thought it was a good idea. When I was little we had various dogs, and they were fun. I thought it would be fun again. I got him – very ethically, I felt – from the RSPCA in Halifax at the end of the summer, following the course change debacle of my first university year. I was spending the break at Alice's, due to move back into the Nook on my return to Sheffield. At the time I was reading the obligatory unofficial students' handbook, Tolkien's *Lord of the Rings,* for the second time, so, naturally, the dog was named Frodo Baggins, later shortened to Frod, Froddy, Baggs, etc.

My grandmother was not pleased by my acquisition. Cute though he was, the new puppy – a mixture of Labrador and something skinny that gives him an athletic adult shape – wreaked havoc on her poor little house. If left alone too long, he rampaged over tables, window sill, sideboard, knocking over teacups, plants, and the small ornaments my grandmother collected and displayed everywhere. A trail of devastation followed his charging little body and fervently wagging tail; chewing shoes and slippers was a particularly favourite pursuit. After a few weeks, to Alice's immense relief, I returned with him to Sheffield.

He's bigger now, of course, and fully house trained – surprisingly easily, compared to previous pups I've known. He fits into the routine of the house straight away. After his initial puppy hysteria, he proves to be exceptionally calm and sharply intelligent. He quickly and easily learns all the usual stuff: sit, stay, lie down, etc, and in my libertarian, egalitarian, student mode, I vow never to teach him inane and useless 'roll-over' type tricks.

History of a Daft A'porth

He's affable, too; everyone in the house takes to him. He's not noisy, he doesn't get in the way, and he has a peaceable character that endears him even to non dog-lovers.

Of course, when I got him, it never occurred to me to consider what I would do with a dog when I went to lectures.

So what *shall* I do?

Hey, this is the seventies. Everything's different. Rules are made to be broken. We're rebels!

He'll come with me...

The first time I take him to a lecture, it's sociology, in a fairly large lecture hall in the Arts Tower. There are around thirty students in the group, and as the dog and I slope in like characters from the infamous *Oz* magazine – every inch the long-haired, bearded, cool guy with his equally cool four-legged companion – there's a chorus of different reactions, roughly matched to the spectrum of coolness across the class. It ranges from from the fawning to the slightly outraged. There are still – despite the zeitgeist of the times – a few uptight, clean-cut types and Young Conservatives, for whom this is criminal behaviour. Only guide dogs allowed, don't y' know!

I take my seat in the middle of the row, and get Frodo to lie down at my feet. If he gets restless, I'll just have to take him out. The prof arrives, and starts his lecture. Frodo stays quietly at my feet throughout, and only gets up when we prepare to leave the lecture theatre. He trots to the end of the row, and waits in the aisle for me to catch up. Only then does the lecturer spot him.

"Has he been here all the time?"

"Yep."

"Well! Goodness, he's well behaved, isn't he?"

"He is."

"Mmm..."

That was it. No further comment. Similar reactions occurred in my philosophy and politics lectures. Maybe the lecturers are, or are trying to be, as right on as their students? I don't take him to every lecture, but he comes along often enough to become a feature, trots into the room, and without being told, ensconces himself in a corner down at the front of the class. He eventually achieves the ultimate accolade: being greeted by lecturers with a "Hello, Frodo," to which he responds with a lugubrious look and a wag of the tail, before curling up into his habitual doggy-donut-long-term-waiting-shape in his usual corner. "He's better educated than most of you lot," quips one professor.

Compliant though he is in these environments, Frodo proves, pretty much from the outset, that, although a stoic and loyal companion, he is very much his own dog. It very soon becomes clear that he when he does what you tell him, it's because he judges that, on balance, it's the right thing to do. He does not – as do most other dogs – exude that air of delighted willingness to obey. If he feels like lying down in the corner when you tell him, he'll do so without hesitation. If, on the other hand, he'd rather be following some more interesting canine pursuit, you'll get the 'look,' an expression on his doggy face that can only be described as 'Oh, alright... if I really *have* to..." accompanied by his highly expressive sigh! He *sighs*... he does! He'll comply, but protest has been duly lodged.

This does not mean he causes problems through capricious disobedience, it simply means he has an opinion on the subject.

For example, training him to close doors takes a little longer than usual. This is not a trick! When you pass from one room to another, – especially in our cold student house – leaving a door open causes a draught. Frodo occasionally comes into a room by himself, and I would like him to shut the damn door after himself like everyone else! So I set about it. It's harder than usual, because I can tell he sees no good reason for it. He doesn't feel draughts; why does he have to do this silly thing of putting his front paws up on the door to shut it? I get the *look*; the "Aw, come on, really?" look, and the *sigh*, until he finally gets it, thank goodness, drops the attitude, and accepts the inevitable. Of course, it becomes a source of raised eyebrows, and 'Wows' amongst our friends when he's reminded of this duty in our or in their houses. But it is *not* a trick! We do *not* do tricks! We do practical; perversely, that can lead to stuff that *looks* like tricks. It can also become the stuff of legend, and consequently Frodo will achieve far more fame – though sadly not fortune – than I ever shall.

I have to admit here to yet another of those decisions of which I am not hugely proud. This independence of spirit Frodo shows makes him a very uncommon creature. He's incredibly composed, and able to wait patiently for sustained periods, such as the lectures. He does, though, love to be out. Not simply in the park chasing a ball or just running – which he loves, and at which he is very quick (I suspect his Labrador is crossed with greyhound) – but just...out. He sometimes just wants to leave the house, and barks politely but insistently at the door to indicate this. My decision is this. I can't always take him out with me, and if we're all out of the house, it's cruel to leave an active dog on its own for extended periods. I have to make the choice, then; do I leave him locked up, or do I let him go out on his own, with all the associated dangers? I've spent considerable time and energy teaching him about traffic; stopping at kerb edges, and making him aware of vehicles. I've walked many miles of urban streets with him, judging his traffic sense, and – once again – my over stimulated youthful hippy libertarianism has played a role: I decide to allow him out on his own. This is a choice I do not make lightly, and it causes me much anxiety in following years. Fortunately, my gamble appears to pay off, and he will survive to rule his various patches for many years. Only much, much later will I really come to regret it.

For now, he's free. He barks to leave, and when he returns, he barks to be let in. He has his rounds, I discover. My musician friend, Dave, later of Rag Revue fame, in whose flat Frodo and I have passed many an hour over coffee, beer, or other stimulant, tells me that Frodo has paid him a visit. "Oh?" I say. "Yes," he replies. Apparently, Dave gets a bark outside his door, and on opening it, there's Frodo. "Hello," says Dave. The dog gives him a wag, enters, and curls up on the rug in front of the fire. He stays for half an hour or so, while Dave does the washing-up and reads for a bit. Then Frodo gets up, goes to the door, and barks for out. Dave opens up, dog gives him another wag, and off he goes. "Bye Frodo."

I'm amused, but not hugely surprised. I've only recently heard even better! I've a Frodo story that will top his.

The dog accompanies me to the students' bar on a regular basis when I drop in for a pint or a game of billiards or whatever, and he's become a well-known face around the union. We often go there and back on the bus – a double decker. It's about three stops, and if it's busy, to keep him out from under careless feet I get him to jump up on the waist-high luggage rack near the stairs at the front. He'll calmly stay curled up there like a furry black bag till we get off, even if I can't get a seat near him.

"Saw Frodo on the bus today." My psychology course-mate, Christine.

"On the bus?"

"Yes, he went to the union."

"What d'you mean he went to the union?"

Christine elaborates. She had been on the 95 bus, which passes the Nook and goes into the town center via the university. It pulled up at the stop nearest our house, the driver opened the doors, and a couple of people got on, followed by Frodo, who hopped up onto the luggage rack, as usual. These are the days when councils run the buses, and there are conductors to take the fares. He came down the stairs from where he had been collecting on the upper deck, and spotting Frodo, asked, "Whose is this dog?" No-one answered, and he was a bit nonplussed. By now the bus was approaching the right stop for the students' union, and at this point, Frodo jumped down and stood waiting at the doors. No-one else got up, but it was obvious the dog wanted off at the next stop, so, with a 'what else can I do' shrug, the conductor rang the bell, the driver pulled up, the doors opened, and Frodo got off.

Although Christine didn't follow him, she can tell me the rest of the dog's tale (sorry!) she heard from a friend.

After getting off the bus, our boy trots along to the students' union. He goes down the stairs into the bar, plants himself in front of the food counter section, tips his head on one side in the way dogs do, and gazes earnestly at the serving ladies until one of them comes out from behind the counter, gives him a pat on

History of a Daft A'porth

the head, a quick cuddle, and a meat pie. After chilling in the bar for a while, he catches the bus back home.

It seems he does this on a not-infrequent basis, and has become celebrated for it. Legend has it that bus drivers now halt even if it's just him waiting at the stop. Christine's account is the first I've heard about this little lunch outing of his, but by now, nothing that wily old mutt gets up to surprises me.

He eventually becomes so well known around the university and the students' union that he's greeted by name wherever he goes. He's adored not only by the food ladies, but also by those arbiters of law and order in the union building – Ray, Frank, and Les, our long-suffering but genial porters in the porters' lodge. They always fuss delightedly over him when we go in. Finally, after several years of patrolling, visiting, and making friends, his exploits (such as the bus riding), eventually make it into the student newspaper, and such is his reputation and the affection in which he's held by staff and students alike, that it's moved one day, in a committee meeting of student council, that he be made a member of the students' union. When an objection is made by certain reactionaries in an attempt to enforce the 'No dogs permitted in the Union' rule, a second motion is proposed and rapidly seconded... to make him an honorary cat...

Both motions are unanimously passed (apart from the roundly mocked objectors), and Frodo is anointed with honorary feline status. Supplied with a suitable photo – taken by proud owner and friend (me) – the following day, the students' union office presents him with his very own custom-made membership card. It's a miniature, disk-shaped union card, laminated, and bears his name, photo, membership number, and the signature of the secretary of the union. This, he sports henceforth on his collar. Should his legitimate entry to the union building be challenged, he has his card. There will be many a stunned dog-owner refused entry by a porter as Frodo simultaneously trots in to a cheery "Hello Frodo" from the very same porter, and heads down to the bar for his pie. The explanation, "Oh, Frodo? He's a union member and honorary cat, sir," usually leaves them speechless.

Many legends will circulate about him in the years to come – how he can ride sat between the arms of a motorcyclist; how he navigates on his own five miles across traffic-thronged London; how, on the pavement outside our house, he plants himself, growling, paws firmly planted in defense over the four kittens he lives with, when his best doggy mate goes for them; how his calm and gentle nature can convert even the most terrified cynophobe into his adoring pal; plus many other stories worthy of a Hollywood movie. Of all the friends I have, and will have, Frodo is the most remarkable, the truest, and the most unchanging. He will be with me throughout my student years and my continued life in Sheffield, and will eventually accompany me when I have to move away. His character and reputation will become a fixture in my various social circles, and without fail his name will be fondly mentioned in future years when I reunite with old friends. His eventual, and despite my efforts, unexplained, disappearance at the age of thirteen will leave me grieving and guilt-ridden, and I will never have another canine companion.

But the love and companionship of a true friend can't prolong the years of academia beyond their natural run, and much as I try to think of excuses for staying on, my university studies are over.

History of a Daft A'porth

Chapter 10: Get a Job!

> And what is it to work with love?
> It is to weave the cloth with threads drawn from your heart
> *Kahlil Gibran*

At least I have a degree: a 2.2. – ironically known as a "Gentleman's Degree. This, according to academic lore, shows you've not wasted your time with too much studying, but have rounded your education, and expanded your horizons with other pursuits... Well, I've certainly done that! But now I need a job. I have to pay the rent somehow. There's no way I'm going back to Halifax!

I'm not a stranger to work. As well as my paper rounds and the pseudo work I did on the boats, I've had a job during most of the long summer holidays every year since I was sixteen. I also spent those backbreaking few weeks on the building site while I struggled to persuade the authorities to let me back into university.
I know about hard graft.

My first crack at what you might call real work, was during that turbulent year of freedom when I turned sixteen. I went around the local factories, asking if they were taking on for the summer. I got a result at Hattersleys' Valves just down the road from my gran's, where I was living, having left home. The factory made valves for fluid systems, and had its own foundry; a Dantean cave of roaring furnace mouths, flame tinged smoke, and gushing hot metal. I was put here as a mould cracker. I had to help break open the cooled sand-filled moulds in which were cast the valve bodies. Valves ranged in size from tiny ones of a few millimeters bore, up to massive ones of two or three hundred millimeters that it took two of us to lift. We broke the moulds open with sledgehammers, and the contents tumbled out, still steaming, and giving off a smell that was the very essence of the

Inferno; coke, smoke, flame, and hot sand, all mixed into one. It was both harsh and thrilling at the same time!

From there I was moved into the testing bay. All the castings, once assembled, had to be integrity tested on great rotating carousells. These valve-festooned roundabouts turned lazily and endlessly in their part of the factory floor, exuding the milky coloured water forced through them at several atmospheres pressure, like weird, lactating mechanical mammals. Failures would cause sudden bubbling streams of this milk to vomit into the collecting tray of the carousell, and the offending valve would be removed and sent back for adjustment. Unfortunately, my job, along with many others on that shop floor – final assembly before the engineers bolted the units to the carousells – was tediously repetitive and crushingly boring. It involved not much more than attaching one part to another with a spanner; the same action over and over again, then adding the completed units to a collecting bin. It was my first taste of the kind of monotony that many types of job demand. One of my workmates, Roland, a man then in his sixties, had been working there for forty years, twenty-five of them on this same job. I stared at him incredulously when he told me this, but, gentle soul that he was, he just smiled wryly and said 'You get used to it.' I vowed then and there never to be trapped in this way when I eventually went to work full time.

It does not occur to me until much older, and just the tiniest fraction wiser, that my success in this vow involves acceptance of a system that condemns those less persistent and less fortunate than me to carry out the tasks I wish so vehemently to avoid. I had not at that age encountered the ideas of the likes of Adam Smith, John Maynard Keynes, or Karl Marx, and was quite happy to wish these doleful occupations onto other people!

The following summer, I went back to the same place, but this time was assigned to the warehouse. I got the impression they didn't actually need anyone, but were generously taking on one or two schoolkids as a kind of social endeavour.

History of a Daft A'porth

As a result, I was left completely alone, with instructions to stock-take all the various sizes and types of valves – each in its own separate cubby hole in the warehouse – and to enter the results in a record book (no computers then!). The factory sold most of its valves on a fairly regular basis, which meant that in reality there weren't very many to count, so I had a lot of spare time on my hands. All of the cubby holes were large enough to sit inside, and I very soon learned that if I climbed up to the third or fourth row, I could safely ensconce myself within one, and read a book without fear of discovery, for several hours at a time. If anyone did come by, either I kept silent and hidden till they passed, or I was 'checking that bin.' I spent the whole summer doing very little factory work, but getting through a pile of fiction and prep for university! When I left, subtle hints were dropped by the warehouse foreman suggesting he knew what I'd been up to, but as long as 'Management' didn't know, it was OK! Fairly typical of the state of industrial relations of the period.

Although I never had it so easy again, the following summer job was possibly the best I've ever had.

At the time, my mother worked at Crossley's' Carpets in Halifax, and put a word in for me. Along with another lucky student temp, I got a place as order-filler while the regular employees were on holiday. Our job was to take orders sent from the sales office, for cut lengths of broadloom carpet, transfer the roll to the cutting machine, which then measured, cut the length, rolled and bagged it. We would send the package off to dispatch, and return the remainder of the roll to its rack.

These broadloom rolls were massive: twelve feet wide with a maximum diameter of around four feet. They lived on racks four tiers high that could be pulled out on their rollers, like library shelves, into a central aisle. To transport the rolls needed small, agile, but powerful, fork-lift trucks. And we got to drive them!

In the words of *Madness*, Oh, what fun we had!

After initial training and supervision, it was obvious we'd quickly got the hang both of driving the trucks and of the order system, and as the mill was short-staffed owing to holiday leave, we were left to get on with it. Driving a fork-lift isn't as hard as it may sound, and we rapidly became the Lewis Hamiltons of the cutting room. After about a week we'd perfected the 'move' for when an order came in. This entailed the following frenetic sequence.

Race to your truck like a Battle of Britain Spitfire pilot; speed towards the appropriate rack; leap off as you approach the rack, and heave it out in front of the slowing truck; leap back on, set the forks simultaneously climbing and inclining forwards to neatly insert between the supports, and under the moving roll of carpet; as you lift the roll from the still sliding rack, start the truck reversing out, and deliver the carpet to the cutting machine hopper before the rack comes to a halt. All this in one smooth, rapid blur of motion. Once cut, the carpet is returned to its place in an equally slick reversal of this operation. Poetry in motion.

When we weren't filling orders, we were racing the trucks, or using them to bash the big, wheeled, fibre-glass waste bins; sending them careering down the central aisles in a kind of crazy mechanized shove-ha'penny game. I shall always recall this as the happiest summer job I've ever had. It was like having your own private set of dodgems, never having to get off, and getting paid for it!

My mother was also responsible for getting me another unusual job. In the late sixties she waitressed in the local branch of the steakhouse chain Berni Inns, and got me a place there as a wine waiter – at sixteen! I learnt how to open bottles at the table, smooth talk diners into buying the Chateauneuf du Pape, mix liqueur coffees, swan around in my white jacket and bow tie, and other useful skills...

In exile in England in 1871, Louis Napoleon III – Bonaparte's grandson – bizarrely claimed his greatest talent was the ability to carve ham thinner than anyone else. In 1968 my proud (and equally ludicrous) boast was the ability to carry sixteen stem glasses threaded into the fingers of one hand like a bulbous chandelier, and pick up ten more in the other: a trick I would

History of a Daft A'porth

continue, albeit rarely, to demonstrate to an admiring public for decades after giving up my 'sommelier' status.

I also worked on the dustbins, in the days before they had mechanical lifts on the back. For the first week or so, I staggered about painfully and inadequately trying to lift stinky, very full metal dustbins from ground to shoulder, and tip them elegantly into the back of the waste lorry. My shambolic early attempts were a source of great amusement to the regulars, who had obviously seen this kind of thing many times. However, as most ugly ducklings do, I eventually blossomed, and achieved the desired swan status amongst my colleagues, trotting round at speed, skillfully manipulating the bins so that we could all finish the allotted round early, and adjourn to the pub. During the happy weeks spent with these hard-working but tremendously cheerful crews, I was often reminded of the famous 'pig men' of my childhood, and their cheery greetings for the children who ran after them on their rounds.

My final holiday jobs come during my last years as a student in Sheffield, and these are at the same time the toughest, the most illuminating, and the most lucrative of all.
Bachelors foods, in the Wadsley Bridge area of the city, dries fresh peas and beans in the summer. It's a short but frenzied period of picking, transporting, processing, and packaging. The peas are harvested first, then the beans, the whole factory seeming to undergo a kind of swivel from one to the other halfway through the summer. Lots of students are taken on, and a species of sub-community grows within the factory, sometimes getting on famously with the regulars, sometimes not. Our jobs are rotated between picking, drying, and packaging. For those lucky ones studying Chemistry or the like, there's the plum job of quality control in the labs. This elite band appears to do very little except swan into the factory in their white coats, take the odd sample of the product, and disappear again.
Beyond this apparent sinecure, packaging is the easiest job. It involves little more than watching the high-speed machines

dropping measured loads into bags, and sealing them; all almost faster than you can follow. The only intervention needed is to clear the occasional jam. If you're at it long enough, it can hypnotise you into a stunned and wide-eyed trance.

The worst job here, from the point of view of tedium, is picking. Not picking off the vine: you sit at a conveyor belt, which passes a constant green river of peas in front of you and your belt-mates. Your job is to pick out any twigs, leaves, stones, or other debris. As students we often get this duty if we want overtime. Four hours of continuously rolling legumes. It is soul-destroyingly boring; infinitely more so than my previous tedium of valve assembly. Again, I can only hope I'm never consigned to this numbing pursuit as a full-time job, and I feel genuine, if uncomfortable, concern for those who are – sometimes for most of their working lives.

Fortunate fillers-in that we are, we get moved around a bit more than the regulars. The prime spot is on the dryers. The shed in which they're housed is a vast cavern filled with three descending lines of huge metal trays, each approximately three metres long and two wide, that process the peas. There are around ten trays to a line, each with a perforated floor allowing hot air to rise through the peas (the ambient temperature in the shed is around 55C). Each tray slightly overhangs the next down the line, and every five minutes or so, they all vibrate clamorously, shaking the peas from tray to tray, dehydrating them more and more as they go. At these moments the drying shed is filled with the judder and crash of these mechanical convulsions as if an express train and a pneumatic drill have given birth to manic clattering offspring. Add in the tropical heat, and in its own way – like the foundry – it's Dantean.

Our job is to rake the peas into even layers, and to ensure there are no back-ups or overflows. When they reach the end of the lines, they decant into huge metal bins, are tested for moisture content by our scurrying white-coated lab rats, then go off to packaging. The cacophony is constant. Eight-hour shifts; twelve, with overtime. You spend so long in the oppressive heat that you lose high levels of salt through sweating, and this has to be

History of a Daft A'porth

replenished. The remedy is by drinks fountains stationed at various points – the most popular in the cooler air outside – that dispense fruit squash... generously salted.

The first time you try it, even though you've lost salt working, it is truly vile. You can't believe that anyone could stomach the vast quantities that the 'veterans' who've already been here a week or so seem to consume. Bit by bit, of course, the body and taste buds adapt, until it seems so normal, so refreshing, that a drink of ordinary, salt-free squash elicits a reaction of wincing distaste; the offending drink spat out on the floor, or if politeness demands, swallowed with all the reluctance of a three-year old downing cod liver oil.

We spend four weeks on rotating shifts working the peas.

Then it's bean season. Green beans in huge bunches are deposited from the lorries onto the top belt of two picking levels. Here, we students spend the first part of the bean season. It's not as bad as the pea picking belts, or the lower bean belts. On our upper belt, as the beans are tipped, they rush along from left to right, and we, like post-office sorters, dispatch them, via equally-spaced 'gates' that we shove vigorously back and forth, into the snibbers. These are great perforated rotating drums that cut the beans from their stalks – and from which they're decanted onto the lower picking belts running away at right angles from our upper one. On both levels– as with the peas – we're supposed to remove debris. This comprises twigs, stones and miscellaneous rubbish, but, unlike with the peas, there's also the occasional bird, killed by the – presumably more voracious – bean harvester. There's even the odd macerated rabbit.

We on the top belt, of course, take huge pleasure in the traditional pursuit, of lobbing these dead birds or rabbits over the snibbers, down onto the lower belts, causing variously chaos, screams, and appalling invective! It lightens the shift, and generally all is forgiven. We all know that at some point in the not too distant future the roles will doubtlessly be reversed.

The other tasks with the beans are pretty much the same as with the peas, except the temperature in the drying shed is a further six degrees C hotter, and the cages shake for longer each time! Beans, unlike peas, don't roll.

The two seasons combined last almost the full length of the university summer vacation: six weeks or more; eight-hour normal shifts plus four hours regular overtime; seven days a week; rotating morning, afternoon, and night shifts week on week. It's punishing, and like the bins, particularly cruel during the acclimatising period. The changeover from night to morning shift, with only a few hours between to recuperate, is more brutal still, leaving most bleary eyed and half-asleep for their first few changeovers; it's amazing there aren't more accidents. Anyway, I survive; thrive, even. It's a great atmosphere with all the other students there, and so lucrative that I come back the following year. And this second stint gives me my first up-close-and-personal experience of union power.

As we know, I don't react well to authority, and there's lots of it about in the work place, some well used, quite a lot of it, not. One of my less-endearing characteristics is my big mouth when it comes to being told what to do. It seems that during that first summer at Bachelors, I earned myself a reputation with management as a bit of a 'troublemaker.' In other words, I wasn't afraid to speak out if I thought that we were being asked to do something unreasonable, or to push for better working conditions. When I apply for the same job the second time around, I'm told I'm not welcome. For every summer job I've had in a large organization, we students have been 'invited' to join the relevant union, and most are glad to do so. Bachelors is no exception. Working with people for a long time, you hopefully make friends, and during the first summer there I worked alongside many of the regulars, some of whom became good mates, and one or two of whom – luckily for me – are union reps. When I'm refused work, I immediately get in touch with one of them. This is a time when Margaret Thatcher's attack on the unions is just beginning, but has not yet wreaked the havoc that it later will on industrial communities throughout the land; the unions still hold a few powerful cards. Unions are paradoxically very like governments; if run by sensible people, with humanity, respect for all, and a capacity to listen to others' points of view, they're generally a force for good and for progress. Run by ideologues with bigoted views and closed minds, they're catastrophes waiting to happen – which is pretty much what eventually will come to pass in Britain in the eighties, when government, management, and unions suffer from parallel dogma-driven leadership. I never get a sense of that head-butting conflict at Bachelors, and there are no strikes during my times there. Instead, there seems to be reasonable détente between union and management, and plenty of give and take. As evidenced by management's subsequent agreement to give me my second term on the peas and beans! I'm grateful to the union for supporting me, it reinforces my belief that they're an essential, and integral part of the national balance. The later tragedies of Orgreave, Maltby, and the like, where pitched battles took place between masses of striking miners and thousands of police, and the eventual Tory evisceration of the union movement in Britain will leave me deeply upset.

I can't be that much of a troublemaker: I work so hard it impresses management sufficiently to promote me to Charge Hand. The merciless treatment I subsequently receive from my fellow student workers reminds me of my building-site days!

Twelve-hour shifts and seven-day-weeks for six to eight weeks earn what for me is a relative fortune! Enough to have a decent holiday at the end of the Bachelors gig, and to buy my first car – we don't count the schoolboy Cortina disaster and a later crappy Robin Reliant – a shiny blue second-hand Morris Marina. And, after four years, my university course is over. Expected or not, it's a bit of a shock.

So... No excuses; I have to find a 'proper' job!

Fate seems to have intervened. Someone I've met through friends works for local government, and sets me up with an interview with one of his contacts. Sheffield District Council have a post coming up for a careers officer. I am, first of all, amazed that Sheffield *has* a careers office, and secondly – given my personal experience of careers advice – I'm struck by the irony of applying for the post. I do, however.

The interview goes surprisingly well. Because of my extensive experience with Student Reception: advising school students, organising conferences, etc, and my psychology degree, I am, they tell me, the ideal candidate. Shortly afterwards I receive a letter offering me the post. It's like a dream. As far as I'm concerned this is the perfect job. I'm to start in two months' time.

Two weeks before the start date I receive another letter from them.

"Owing to budget cuts, the current financial situation... blah blah... the salary for the post is no longer available. Our abject apologies, but... etc. etc."

My God... I'm out of the job before I even start it!

What on earth do I do now?

"Why don't you try teaching?" Various people ask in various different ways. Maybe that's not a bad idea.

But I know nothing about teaching. One would expect a person who has spent sixteen years being educated by that profession to have picked up at least some idea of how it works. Not so. In fact, I suspect that school and university students are the least qualified of all to understand teachers and teaching, spending as they do, so much of their time either trying to avoid lessons, or bad mouthing those who deliver them.

Despite this unpromising outlook, I apply for, and get, a one-year post-grad place at Totley Teacher Training College on the outskirts of Sheffield, and – once again, astonishingly – a full grant for it. This is the last one, they tell me: I've used up the full quota!

And indeed, it is one of the last for anyone. The end of an era is in sight. For all students. What is looming is the erosion of equal opportunity of education for all, and the reintroduction of the classic elitist ideal: better education for those who can afford it. The policy of student loans, made necessary by ideologically reduced taxation that can no longer support the grants system, will plunge thousands into unnecessary debt before their thirties, will discourage thousands of others from going on to further education through fear of debt, face parents with terrible dilemmas about whether they can afford to support their children at college, and will even affect young people's ability to afford housing.

We now, are the blessed generation; we've been allowed the gift of true social mobility through enlightened educational and social policies. Our rulers accept that paying for our complete education is an investment that benefits the whole nation, therefore the whole nation should foot the bill. The returns far outweigh the costs. But we're the last ones. Ideals will be sacrificed on the altar of fiscal policy and short-termism. Education will become a commodity. We baby boomers are lucky, yet right now we're oblivious of our good fortune; we have no concept that things might ever change, and we accept the precious gift of higher education as our God-given right. It's no wonder that future generations of students, our own children amongst them, will look back on this as a golden age with a mayfly span; a shining ephemeral example, snuffed out like a candle.

Totley college is weird. Or so it seems to me. I've spent four years at university in the hotbed socio-political climate of the early seventies, and here it's like stepping back in time. They're all so young! And so dull! It's as though every interviewee from my Student Reception days has been scooped straight from school and delivered to this campus. We postgrads strut about the place like Norse gods amongst mortals. We are ostentatiously bohemian, flaunting our 'life experience' in the faces of these ingenues. Playing the elder statesman card, I manage to get myself elected chairman of the student council, and have a great time ruling my particular little roost for a year. The students' union officers are unpaid, apart from Diane, the secretary, who's a full-time employee. She's very pretty, funny, and smart, with gorgeous long red hair, and I quickly fall under her spell. It soon transpires, after a few evenings in the union bar, that there's a mutual attraction. Diane will turn out to be one of my heart-breakers, as right from the start she's torn between me and her 'ex' boyfriend. We have ten months of stormy, triangular tug of war, often tearful on both our parts, and eventually, as I near the end of my course, she'll go back to him.

The course, I find manageable, and I even draw on my psychology background for the academic side. Eventually though, we have to go on teaching practice. Everybody dreads this, including we cocky post-grads, and it turns out to be just as terrifying as expected. Not because the kids are awful; they are in fact, mostly lovely, but because we feel utterly without expertise. I'm so cool, with my long hair and my George Harrison moustache and beard, but I haven't got a clue! We're all adrift, muddling through as best we can and hoping not to make too many terrible mistakes. Somehow, we all make it, goodness knows how!

One great thing about my own teaching practice is that for the second batch, at the end of the year, I have to commute to and from school in the tiny Derbyshire village of Great Longstone, on my 1970 650cc Bonneville, through the beautiful hills and valleys of the peak district. It's worth it just for the drive.

These last weeks in a school turn out to be not so bad. The kids seem to like me, I've finally learned enough to be able to run lessons, and the staff seem happy to leave me to it. I even coach the cricket team, putting its eleven-year-old captain straight as to how to manage his team more empathetically, and not shout at them so much!

I could do this.

But in the end, I don't.
For two reasons.
First, despite passing my course, and qualifying to teach, I'm unconvinced I want to do this; more than that, I'm convinced I *don't* want to do this.
Secondly, something else gets in the way.
Go-Dangle...
Who...?...

History of a Daft A'porth

Chapter 11: Greasepaint: 1 – Foundation

All the world's a stage, and all the men and women merely players
  Jaques: Shakespeare's As You Like It

During my time at university, The Nook's population remains reasonably stable; the majority staying put for several years. One or two changes take place – the love-triangle incident famously splitting up the Nook Band, of course, but we also have the occasional transient, who moves in for a few months, and then gets their own place. One of these is Bob's friend Macca.
John MacDonald (Macca) and Bob went to school together in the Co. Durham steel town of Consett. Bob came to university, and Macca went to work in the steel mills. Along with a common childhood, they share a love of folk music. Bob plays guitar (very well) and sings, Macca just has his voice – which is a very good, powerful, Geordie folk singer's voice. Having stayed in touch with Bob, and eager to taste life beyond his home town, he comes to visit, and after staying on our sofa for a few weeks, officially moves in. He soon joins the Nook band, and he and I do some singing at local folk clubs. Macca is one of those people who, despite their lack of formal education, have a formidable thirst for knowledge and a passionate drive to explore the world around them. He's hugely energetic, and never still.
"Hey Pete mun, you should give this a go!" His rich Consett accent precedes him as he enters the house. "Ah've been helping out at this club, like, in town. It's for young-uns... keep em off the street, like. Ah know the bloke what runs it. It's council, an' they're reet tight with money, an' he could do w'y a hand. D'y fancy helpin uz owt like?"
Apparently, Macca has met Charlie through a folk club. Charlie is a youth worker for Sheffield social services, and runs a club for adolescents in the town, not far from the students' union. Short of volunteers, he asked Macca if he fancied helping, and Macca – always eager for new experiences – agreed. Now he's down there every week, and he says it's such 'good craic' that I should come too. And Charlie really needs the help. Somewhat

reluctantly, but as is often the case, bedazzled by Macca's charm and enthusiasm, I accompany him.

The youth club is unlike any I've ever seen before. It takes place in a couple of rooms in what looks like an empty shop with a toilet and basic kitchen facilities, on the edge of the city centre. Charlie is about forty, avuncular, and dynamic. His brood of about twenty kids range from around ten to sixteen years. What fascinates me, and over the course of the first visit, draws me in like iron filings to a magnet, is how Charlie runs the sessions.

It's called improvisation. After a bit of settling in at the start of the evening, Charlie organises a few what he calls 'games,' which consist of circles or pairs of kids using voice or movement in such activities as passing silent messages, manipulating a fictitious object, mirroring movements in slow motion, constructing a human assembly line to make an imaginary product, and various other tasks designed to unlock the kids' creative powers. They then split into groups – each adult joining one – and every group is given a word or a phrase. There's a set time period to develop a scenario – an improvisation – to illustrate in some way the word or phrase. Charlie doesn't stick to convention in his phrases; my group gets, for example, "The door in the neck of the giraffe." Each group subsequently performs its improvisation to the others, often to gales of laughter. The sessions last from around seven till nine pm, and run once a week. The kids obviously love it.

It doesn't take more than one or two visits, and I'm hooked. Not only is it fun, but amazingly, I discover I've a knack for it: for improvisation... for taking an idea, and creating something from it that others find interesting, and even entertaining! I can take on character, pretend effectively to be someone not myself. I've discovered, effectively, that I can act!

I become a regular helper, and at Christmas that same year, the group devise, script, and put on a pantomime, funded by the council, and attended by a real audience (mostly the kids' parents). I'm the wicked Sir Jasper, with my top hat and my

History of a Daft A'porth

cloak. The audience willingly and enthusiastically jeer, hiss, and boo when I come on stage. I'm happier than I knew possible.

Inevitably, depressingly, and despite the obvious social contribution the group is making to the local community, the council, in their wisdom – or perhaps in the straits induced by cuts in government funding – wind it up, and the kids are unceremoniously dumped on the streets again.

Plus ça change!

What becomes of Charlie, I never discover. I can only hope that all concerned benefit from the short life of this innovative and creative group as much I have. Because, having unearthed this new passion, I crave some other way to satisfy the lust I now have to take to the stage.

The next logical step, therefore, is to join University Theatre Group.

Theatre Group is a students' union society that does pretty much what it says on the tin. It puts on plays. Most of these are truly appalling. Some, however, are quite good. The odd one or two are very good.

I throw myself into the action, auditioning for every production. And I get cast. At first, it's because there's a sort of 'everybody gets a go' attitude, but eventually I start to get main roles. Whatever my *actual* talent, I *believe* myself to have some, and confidence can be the deciding factor in this. People begin to tell me I can do this acting thing quite well, and that pushes me to try even harder. It's a stubborn part of my nature that whatever I do, I push myself to do it as well as I possibly can. This isn't always feasible, of course; some skills are beyond some of us. Succeed or not, the intention's there, and I set about learning the craft as best I can. I get book after book out of the library. I watch other, more skilled and knowledgeable colleagues at work acting or directing; I scrutinise the technique of film and stage performers, and I ask questions, questions, questions of fellow actors. I study stage make-up, sound and lighting. Having well and truly invaded my world, theatre, and all that goes with it, becomes a large part of my life, and I throw myself into it in all my spare time. I discover that there are different genres:

Shakespeare of course, Theatre of the Absurd, Classical, Avant Guard, Farce, Physical, Political, etc. and I avidly set about gaining more experience and skills.

I direct my first show – a dramatised reading of Dylan Thomas' *Under Milk Wood*, which seems well received. And – a landmark for any budding actor – I get a good role in my first Shakespeare. A student production, it's nonetheless lavishly done, with a stunning, ruined-castle set, and a production design based on the Sutton Hoo mask. It's Macbeth. I am MacDuff. I get to kill the foul fiend!

As a teenager, going to see Macbeth had been my first visit to the theatre proper (i.e. not pantomimes with my mum). I was in the fifth form at school, and our English department organized the outing; a coach trip to the *Octagon* theatre in Bolton.

It was a thrilling and muscular performance, but one moment in particular stood out for me. At some point in the action, as Macbeth and his entourage left the stage, one of them, having eaten an apple during their scene, accidentally dropped the core on stage as they exited. It lay there, a tiny interloper in the full glare of the lights as the following scene opened and the next set of actors walked on. I could tell that the rest of the audience, as well as I, were transfixed by this small thing, this errant apple core that shouldn't have been there. As they entered, angrily discussing Macbeth's evil doings, one of the actors directed his fury at the apple core, giving it a vicious kick that sent it skimming across the stage and into the stalls, raising gasps of half shock, half delight from the audience. It was just an apple core kicked away, but it was so real, so apt, so... *right*!

I owe this revelatory moment to another inspirational teacher, Mr. Bates, English master at Halifax Technical High School. He encouraged in me an enduring and fervent love of my native tongue, and by taking us to see the play, gifted me with that electrifying apple-core moment that I believe conceived my passion for theatre. This passion, though it lay dormant until awakened by Macca and Charlie, was there and waiting as surely as the blood in my veins, eventually surfacing, and leading implacably to the moment where, as McDuff, I kill Macbeth.

History of a Daft A'porth

And coincidentally, where I also nearly kill a member of the audience.

Over weeks, Kevin (Macbeth) and I have meticulously choreographed the fight between Macbeth and McDuff that takes place near the end of the play. It's short, but violent, involving rushing charges, Macbeth tumbling over my back to the floor, and a swinging, hacking broadsword fight. All goes well for the first few nights. Then one night, suddenly, on one of the ringing clashes of swords we have so carefully rehearsed, mine slices off his blade completely and violently at the hilt, and sends it spinning and humming through the air – straight at the front row of the audience. I hear the same collective intake of breath that I recall so well from the apple-core, and time slows to a crawl as all eyes follow the hurtling shard on its terrifying trajectory.

Thankfully for all concerned, it crashes to a halt on the floor – inches from the feet of the front row. For an eternity there's stunned silence. Macbeth and I catch ourselves staring at each other with a barely disguised 'what do we do now?' actor's face. Incredibly, the spirit of that long-ago witnessed performance of the play seems to take over. The noble McDuff, after a long second of thought, rejects the unfair advantage of his intact broadsword, flings aside his weapon, draws the dagger he (luckily) has at his belt, and he and Macbeth wrestle mightily into the wings. Mentally, I give thanks to that long-ago actor and his inspired kick!

Rag Week is run every year by pretty much every university and college as an excuse to do wildly crazy things (crazy, even for students) in the guise of raising huge amounts of money for charity. I've taken part in many of them myself: beer marathons, overnight charity walks, home-made-raft races on the extensively polluted and junk-filled river Don – before which one has to visit Student Health for a tetanus jab! Part of this week of lunacy (which half the local population love, and the other half loathe), is Rag Revue, a collection of sketches and idiocies loosely making up a show, for which tickets are sold to the student body as part of fund raising. Traditionally, it is derisory. Poorly organized, sloppy, performed by people from Rag Committee, and not particularly funny. Nobody ever wants to take it on, especially those in Rag Committee.

Desperate, this year they approach Theatre Group, and as a newish director I'm asked if I'll take it on. At first, I'm dismissive; Rag Review? Peuh! Then it occurs to me that there might be a chance here to make a mark. To the surprise of my Theatre Group colleagues, I accept the challenge. I have a plan.

If the plan works, *this* year's Rag Revue won't be the unmitigated disaster it usually is; it'll be done properly. It will be *Theatre*.

I audition for actors, and gather a troupe of five or six talented people plus two brilliant musician friends. We set about collecting ideas for sketches. One of these is to use the surprisingly erudite and very, very, funny graffiti that covers every square centimetre of the male and female toilets in the students' union. It's a great source of jokes, political satire, pithy comment, and plain craziness, and on its own it furnishes material for several sketches. We also write our own scripts, being careful to steal only good stuff from elsewhere, and to be as objectively self-editing as possible. The musicians cook up some clever and relevant songs mixing the collected material with their own. After a couple of weeks, we've got enough for the show. What it needs now is pulling into a whole, to draw everything together. This is where the plan is crucial. I write a script for three characters; three 'old geezers' who act as links between the sketches and songs. They start the show with a chat to the audience, reminiscing about when they used to be students here, and, oh what a time they had... etc. They then retire to sides of the stage to watch the actors reliving their student adventures. When there's a gap or a scenery change between sketches, they come back on and blather about the old days, each of the memories triggered by the preceding sketch and leading into the next. Added together they form a narrative, and the whole show culminates with these three degenerates at

History of a Daft A'porth

the end of their tale, singing and dancing a pastiche of *A Policeman's Lot Is Not a Happy One*: our version... *A Flasher's Lot*, etc (same tune), complete with dirty macs and a *full* reveal just before final blackout.

It brings the house down. Standing ovations. Both nights. Huge success. "Never realised Rag Revue could actually be good!" etc

Cast and crew are, as they say where I come from, 'made up.'

It is my first real taste of showbiz accolade and the adrenaline rush that it brings, and I want more.

I'm lucky enough to get more, and I continue to act and direct for theatre group... but it's still just a hobby.

Until I get a tap on the shoulder.

I'm coming to the end of my postgrad year in teacher training, and I'm floundering aimlessly around trying to decide in which direction to look for a career. I'm still acting in various student plays, and it's in the pub next to the university theatre, during an after-show drink, that I'm tapped on the shoulder.

"Hello. Peter? Ed Grist."

"Hello."

"You were very good."

"Oh, thank you." (People compliment actors all the time without really meaning it...)

"No, really, I mean it. Got a minute?"

"What for?"

This is answered by a bit of small talk about the play, then,

"Have you heard of 'Go-Dangle?"

"Go what?"

"The Go-Dangle Trust. We're a T.I.E. company based here in Sheffield"

"T.I.E?"

"Theatre in Education."

"Ohh...?"

"We've just lost an actor – gone back to the States – and we're looking for somebody else, and... Well, we were wondering if you might be interested. We've seen you in a few things now, and we think you'd make a good Go-Dangle member."

"Me?"

"Yes. Could we talk a little bit more about it?"

Absolutely we could talk a little bit more about it! After getting over my initial shock at apparently being head-hunted, I discover more from Ed and his Go-Dangle colleagues. The company was set up by him and a couple of others after a trip to the US, and their involvement with a similarly named company there. It's registered as a charity, which means they can apply for funding to local government, arts, and other bodies, and they pay Equity (actors' union) rates to their actors. They write their own material, and take plays into schools. The American from their company has gone back home, they need a replacement, and... voila, as the French say.

On the face of it, I should leap at the chance. A professional actor! Wary, though, I endure some soul searching before I accept. It's a big risk... a small theatre company... unknown prospects... But I've nothing else to tempt me, and finally I do accept, and in 1973, I become a fully paid-up member of the Go-Dangle Theatre Company.

Go-Dangle is: Chris and Nigel, trustees; Ed, trustee/actor; Jenny, actor and Chris's wife; Richard, actor, and me. Collectively we're responsible for researching and writing scripts, making or sourcing props and costumes, organizing rehearsals, loading and driving the van, and, of course, acting. The trustees handle the money side; raising it, and paying us and expenses. They've managed to get funding from Yorkshire Arts Association and South Yorkshire district council, and this is enough to rent rehearsal space and pay us the Equity minimum grand sum of £60 a week.

It's the start of a five-year journey in professional fringe theatre, and a lifetime of involvement at a semiprofessional or amateur level. It will at different moments be fulfilling, moving, thrilling, sad, combative, stressful, and (thankfully rarely) truly awful.

As a small itinerant company, we're not alone. This is a period of tremendous flowering for small theatre groups, as theatre itself evolves from a traditional form into more experimental and professionally diverse modes. Theatre schools expand; acting

History of a Daft A'porth

itself embraces a wider intake, and tries to reach a broader audience. Hence the appetite for TIE companies.

My first production with Go-Dangle is a myth-buster. Based on the book *Bury My Heart At Wounded Knee* by Dee Brown, we write a play aimed at 9/10-year-olds chronicling the genocide of the Native American peoples by white settlers and their armies. Before each performance, we organise the audience of children sitting in a circle round the playing area into 'tribes,' giving each child in the 'tribe' a simple coloured necklace to wear. At various points during the play, when something terrible happens to the Sioux or Cheyenne during the play, such as a massacre, the breaking of a treaty, or a forced migration, one by one the 'tribes' have to symbolically give up their necklaces. Our aim is to show the real, tragic side of the Cowboys and Indians stories, movies, and games they're exposed to. We seem to succeed. Some of the children are reduced to tears giving back their necklaces (from involvement, not avarice!). They're also thrilled by the fight that takes place in their midst between Sioux brothers, the sensible Joe and hothead Charlie: I as Joe intercept Charlie as he lunges at the 'white man oppressor' (played by Ed) with a hunting knife. Looking back on this with later good sense, I'm appalled at that we did it every time with a real nine-inch-bladed sheath-knife in the middle of a circle of young children!

One would expect that first Macbeth to have taught me something. Apparently not!

Amazingly, not a single teacher ever complains!

Go-Dangle goes on to produce its next myth-busting play on the theme of Robin hood; this one, street theatre, to enlighten the shoppers and passers-by in various Yorkshire towns. The reality is that our legendary hero is probably based on several different, fairly unsavoury, thieves and villains, and didn't really exist. It's during this production that I ride home on the bus dressed in my Sherriff of Nottingham black doublet and hose with a rapier in my belt. Again, not a peep of protest from fellow passengers, and only a wry smile from the conductor as he takes my fare! We have a decade or two to go before Health and Safety...

Peter Benson

After this comes a much more serious piece: *Aberfan*. It will be a difficult and contentious show, and quite out of the blue, its preparation and writing will expose me to one of the most moving experiences of my life.

Aberfan is a multimedia performance for secondary schools, using animation and surround-sound along with the actors, to tell the story of the Welsh village disaster and its aftermath, and to explore the ideas of blame and responsibility.

During lengthy planning discussions, we bang our heads together over the morality of going to Aberfan itself as part of the research for the show. Even though it's ten years since the catastrophe, would it be insensitive, or even ghoulish, to go? On the other hand, could we write about it truthfully *without* going? After a great deal of soul-searching and to-ing and fro-ing, we agree that to be able to write an honest and respectful script, we *must* go. Discreetely.

The date the others fix for their visit, I can't make, so I arrange to go a few days earlier. I hitch-hike most of the way, arrive at the town late evening, and take a room in a B and B. The following morning, after a hearty Welsh breakfast, I set off to the cemetery. This perches starkly on the side of the hill a few yards above the town, not far from where the little primary school was tragically overwhelmed by the cascading monster of the slag heap. As I approach, I can see that as well as the typically solid ancient headstones, there's something different; something stands out.

Halfway up the tiny patch of ground that holds the dead of Aberfan, are two rows, one above the other, of identical, waist-high white stone arches stretching the length of the little graveyard. They are linked together, each spanned to its neighbour with a short horizontal. It's impossible not to be reminded of children holding hands in a line. As I reach the arches, and begin my slow traverse along one row then back along the next, I pass all of the children's names, darkly etched into the white stone. But what affects me, beyond my ability to control, is that here, ten long years after the event, each pale,

History of a Daft A'porth

desperate little arch has a bunch of fresh flowers in front of it. Every one. It's impossible to bear. I reach the end of this avenue of unspeakable tragedy, sit heavily on the low wall, and weep helplessly for a long, long time.

I can hardly bare to share this with my colleagues, it's so painful, and they all undergo similar experiences when they visit. We have to be very careful to ensure the resulting play is not simply an angry rant at the horror and injustice of it all. In the end, as well as saying this must never, ever happen again, we try also to convey that if one seeks to lay blame, then every one of us has to accept at least some. Discussion groups after the shows give us some hope that we've succeeded.

After this we take on other causes that seem to us neglected or misunderstood, and that we feel passionately should be wider known. Minamata, a Japanese fishing community poisoned by film manufacturing effluent, causing appalling birth deformities in the children; the issues surrounding sexism and racism, played out in a life-sized Punch and Judy show; feminism and misogyny examined through a collection of sketches; and many more. Occasionally as a fund raiser, we put on a 'conventional' play – usually a comedy. Thus, I also find myself back playing Irish priests, detective inspectors, and dozy husbands, in small local theatres across Yorkshire, and sometimes as exotically far away as Cheshire!

At some point, irritated by continuing incomprehension and mockery of the company's name, and to try to appear more attractive to local funding sources, we ditch the title *Go-Dangle* (which frankly, I've always regarded as a bit weird!), and dub ourselves *South Yorkshire Theatre Workshop*. By this time, actors have come and gone, and I'm the only original company member left, though Ed and Nigel are still trustees. I have by erosion become principal scriptwriter, props-maker, and frequently, director.

We feel that the company needs a shake-up: some external and more experienced input, so we advertise for a full-time director. Amazingly, as a result of this, we're privileged to work for a few months – until he goes back home – under a recent director of the Toronto theatre, Canada! We learn a lot, not the least of which is some well-needed humility!

The company does well, gaining a reputation for innovative and challenging work. It doesn't pay wonderfully, but we manage. None of us can afford to buy our own home, but we all manage to live in a reasonable gaff. We adore what we do, and put our hearts into it. But theatre's a strange beast. It can eat you up. There are groups like ours who allow the work to absorb them completely. They become insular and over politicized, losing touch with their intended audience, and so failing to get across whatever their message may be. They can become caricatures of themselves. We strive, therefore, not to become isolated luvvies broadcasting agit-prop from our little ivory tower. We won't allow the job to be all-consuming. We deliberately leave time for social lives, and allow ourselves to live in the real world, outside of the imaginary ones we create. We meet friends away from the group, go on holiday. We watch TV. We see the pictures of Mercury from Mariner ten; Richard Nixon resigning after the Watergate affair. The first Apple computer is birthed; Star Wars is released. The world turns.

Sadly, it can't last. In 1979, the cuts in public services instigated by Maggie Thatcher's recently elected Conservative government begin to bite. Little by little at first, and then suddenly, like water disappearing down a sink, our funding disappears. We try everywhere to raise more, but the economic climate is glacial. Unemployment is rocketing, and local government is feeling the pinch. Central government has begun the grinding and relentless degradation of community, culture, and local cohesion that will persist in some form or another for many decades to come, despite the efforts of the 1974-79 Labour government under Wilson and Callaghan. South Yorkshire Theatre Workshop folds, and after five years of hard but incredibly fulfilling work, we go our separate ways.

History of a Daft A'porth

I use the opportunity to visit my mother in Cleckheaton. The atmosphere is alien. But she is delighted to see me – I haven't visited much over the last few years – and fusses relentlessly, cooking favourite meals, and asking lots of questions about work and love life. I've brought Frodo. She has met and grown fond of him on her rare visits to Sheffield, and she lavishes almost as much affection on him as on me.
Fred and I now have an altogether different relationship. Age has made him older and weaker, and he is also ill. At the same time, although no pugilist, I am bigger and stronger. We have a tacit understanding that I am now more than a match for him.
For years I've cultivated the intention to exact revenge of one kind or another for all the tears and anguish he's caused me. I'll call him out, or provoke an argument, and I will thrash him till he begs for mercy.
It never happens.
Spending the last ten years amongst kind, gentle, affectionate, generous friends, colleagues, and lovers has by osmosis given me a certain level of emotional maturity. I no longer feel the need to vent my wrath upon him. I find myself instead harbouring only a kind of scornful pity. Contempt if you wish. At times we occupy the same room but never speak – rarely even look at each other. I'd promised myself again and again that when he died, I would piss on his grave. A few years from now, however, when cancer takes him, I'll feel nothing. As I will find out still later in life, I'm not without baggage from my time under his oppressive rule, but his passing will move me no more than like a distant stone thrown into water; a slight splash, and a few ripples that subside to nothing.
In 1979, though, as I say goodbye again to my tearful mother, and the dog jumps in the car, Fred is still a morose presence in the house, sitting silently, refusing to acknowledge my departure, as he did my arrival and my presence. This brooding, mutual disdain solidifies my conviction that I can never call this place my home, and, I realise now, wherever *he* was has never been a home for me in the true sense of the word. Two hours

later, as Frodo and I walk in the door of our Sheffield house, I feel overwhelmingly and certainly that *this* is my home.
It's good to be back, but...
I'm on the dole.

History of a Daft A'porth

Chapter 12: Snap!

A good photograph is knowing where to stand.

Ansel Adams

An important aspect of theatre – as with any other commercial enterprise – is marketing. Publicity. And of this, a crucial component is photography. I had my first camera when I was ten or so; a battered little second-hand Box Brownie. I took a few rolls of pretty awful holiday snaps, mostly poorly exposed, and with little interest as far as subject matter. When the novelty wore off, the Brownie languished a while in a cupboard, and over several house-moves, disappeared. A few years later, as a teenager, I bought myself a cheap 35mm Zenith SLR, and tried to be arty with it. It didn't last, and the camera was confined to a shelf, except, once again, for the occasional holiday pic or two. For many years, again, I had little or no desire to take anything other than the odd snap of my pals or the dog. And then, halfway through my time with Go-Dangle, my interest is sparked. Adrian, a rotund, bewhiskered, university acquaintance, who processes and prints his own black and white film, asks me to help him in the students' union darkroom. He's taking photos and providing front-of-house prints for student shows, so that in itself is a draw for me.
And once again, a chance discovery, the influence of a friend, something that begins as a naïve fascination, is going to change my life.
Processing and printing black and white film is not difficult, anyone can do it, and I take to it straight away. It has me hooked. I soon become competent, and set up my own home darkroom in my bedroom. I begin taking pictures for Go-Dangle, and then for others involved in theatre: portraits for aspiring actors, images for small commercial projects, etc. After Adrian moves away, I take over doing show pictures for Theatre Group, and selling copies to the casts becomes a small source of extra income. I experiment with colour film, but it's too expensive and difficult to control technically, and I decide to stick to black and

white. It's the beginning of an ardent and enduring love affair with the complex and subtle tones of the monochrome image.
As I did on discovering theatre, I begin to educate myself in the history, technique, and artistry of photography. Like theatre, it's not only fascinating, but beautiful and incredibly diverse. It's a joy to discover its origins, its esoteric mechanics, and the creativity and skill of its best practitioners. Once again, I'm inspired.
All this, though, is a secondary pursuit compared to my theatre career.
Until my theatre career abruptly comes to an end!

Equity is the trade union for the performing arts. Because of a prevailing climate of distrust within its ruling elite, for bolshy little theatre companies like ours and their demands for equal membership rights, we all failed spectacularly to achieve Equity union cards. If you were in a group like ours, you tended to be working full time, and didn't really need a card. Which meant we didn't try to get one until it was too late. In the world of 'conventional' theatre, if you're without a card, it's incredibly hard to get work.
So, now, in 1979, it's even harder than usual to get roles as an actor. And that's not easy even with a card!
If I'm honest, the last few years on the road with South Yorkshire Theatre Workshop have been utterly exhausting, and I feel I need a break from it, so I don't actually make that much effort. At least for a bit. But rent must be paid, groceries bought. My results in the photographic sphere are improving, and to my utter surprise one September day, whilst perusing the jobs section in the local paper, I see an ad for an 'assistant photographer:' *not* a 'photographer's assistant' – which is an altogether different animal: much lowlier! All the more astonishing to find it here and not in the usual place – the British Journal of Photography. Be that as it may, I apply for the job. It should fill in until the acting takes off again.
I'm invited for interview by Andy, the senior photographer. Embarrassingly, and unprofessionally, I don't have a proper

History of a Daft A'porth

portfolio, just a cardboard box full of sample images. I turn up full of hope, but expecting the worst. Andy turns out to be a lovely chap who's the principal photographer for D-Photography, a commercial photography business producing press and advertising images for local firms. He shows me round, looks at my work, and introduces me to the boss, Mr D-. Afterwards, there's the usual 'we'll let you know.'

The following day he does. I've got the job!

I'm stunned. The set up and work he'd shown me were way out of my league in my opinion, and I expected a 'Thank you and goodbye.' Instead he tells me that, despite other candidates having proper art-school style portfolios, my little cardboard box of photos had impressed him the most! Whatever were the qualities that he liked, I don't know, but apparently, I'm now an assistant photographer.

Boy, do I have a lot to learn! Most of the equipment they have here – cameras, lighting etc – is a universe away from my meagre kit. Medium format Yamahas and Hasselblads with interchangeable rotating backs, and a five-by-four-inch Sinar sheet-film bellows studio-camera with rising front, and focal plane tilt. With what? But a machine's a machine, whatever the discipline, and machines can be fathomed; which I do, with the aid of a manual, reasonable quickly. Lighting too. In that domain, I already know some stuff, so I pick up Andy's techniques without trouble. He's good at his job, and also at passing on his expertise, and he gradually gives me more and more responsibility. I do actually start off as a mere photographer's assistant, given that Andy's persuaded the firm to take a punt on someone with little commercial work experience, but I settle in, and I'm given more of my own commissions. Astonishingly, after just a few weeks I become, 2nd photographer. I'm surprised and thrilled about this, 2nd photographer! Who would have thought? Over the next six months I'll learn a huge amount about commercial and industrial photography from Andy – enough of a foundation, in fact, to provide me with a fulfilling career and a good living over the next twenty years: for which I shall be eternally grateful.

Four months in. Mr D- calls me into his office. He wants a chat. It seems the firm needs to make more money. They took me on with the idea of expansion, and it's time I started to help with that. I'm not sure what he means, is my photography not up to scratch? No, no, it's fine, he assures me, it's just they've got to get me generating more revenue.
Alongside the photography, the firm makes small display booths containing an automatic slide projector. These booths can be set up anywhere in business premises, at a conference, or as part of an exhibition stand, hopefully using D- Photography images. From now on it's part of my job to take one of these – 'easily assembled' – booths out with me on jobs, and demonstrate it to the client in the hope of an order. OK, this is new… But, if the boss asks you to do it, you do it.
Soon after, I'm asked to take out the booth to prospective clients even when I'm not taking pictures for them, and progressively, insidiously, this becomes the major part of my job. I've been turned into a sales rep!
I am not good at it. Of course I'm not good at it, I've never had any sales training, and I don't like doing it. So I don't have any success. I do not get a single order. I'm not taking many photos, (because I'm out 'repping!') and then Mr D- says I'm not paying my way. I feel a surge of indignation and anxiety. In my opinion, this is not what I was employed to do, and I feel undermined and cheated. I feel I've been lied to, even. Andy's embarrassed that I've been put in this position, but as an employee himself, he's unable to do anything about it. We plod on this way for another month or so, with me 'not performing,' and becoming more and more demoralised. The bosses (both Mr *and* Mrs D-), become more and more dissatisfied with my contribution – or lack thereof – to the firm's finances.
At the end of my six-month probationary period they 'let me go.' I'm outraged. It leaves me with not only a nasty taste in my mouth, but also a lasting sense of injustice and mistrust in the

History of a Daft A'porth

workplace. From here on I will carry a wariness and suspicion of employers, no matter how nice they appear on the surface.
So, on the dole I go again, but at least, thanks to Andy, I've got some good tools in my kit now, and a proper portfolio at last!

Three months of social security later, I spot an ad in the BJP for a 2nd photographer in a commercial studio. But the job's in London. It would be a great wrench to leave Sheffield, and I'm horribly torn between the need for work, and the affection for what I have come to regard as my home town. I discuss it with Viv, and with my close friends, and they're all of the opinion that such an opportunity shouldn't be sneered at. Reluctantly, I apply, and because this is a London firm, once again I expect not to get it. I go down to The Smoke for an interview in a rather run-down office in the east end, and – once more to my utter astonishment – I get the job. If only I could have known now what I will later find out...

London, including – perhaps especially – its photographers, had grabbed the sixties and seventies by the scruff of the neck, and given them a good shake. Off fell the trappings of a post-war era, and in their place were donned those of the 'Age of Aquarius.' The high-fashion, flared pants and military jackets, mini and maxi skirts, big floppy hats – for men and women – and a whole new libertarian, morally freer, less rigid system came into play. Photography, with its fast-snapping and fast-talking young men, its chic, beautiful models of both genders, and its highly visible profile, was at the head of this thrusting new movement.
Not K- Photography! The sixties have very definitely passed it by, and at the beginning of 1980, are still an irrelevance.
The firm is based in Walthamstow, in East London, and is possibly as far removed from anything remotely resembling Swinging London as it's possible to get. We photograph furniture. This of itself should not necessarily be boring. The advertising shots one sees every day in the media look fabulous; state-of-the-art kitchens, glamourous bedrooms, luxury bathrooms, etc. We, on the other hand, photograph wardrobe

after wardrobe on a white background; sometimes a coloured background (wow!). There are some variations: a chest of drawers, or some shop cabinets; even a small item such as a machine part for an engineering company. But it's mostly wardrobes, wardrobes, wardrobes. Not only is the work tedious and repetitive, but the methods employed appear firmly entrenched in the previous century. When I applied for the job, I didn't have enough experience to suss out fully the environment in which I was going to work. If I'd been more astute and more observant, I would have seen the clues.

The firm is run by two partners, T- and J-.

J-, in his mid-sixties, handles the admin side of the business, and T-, ex RAF, bushily moustachioed and nearly seventy, is the photographer. Nothing at all wrong there, but...

The standard of photography the firm produces is, to say the kindest thing... adequate.

Despite most of our clients being manufacturers of large furniture items, the studio space is not designed for large items! Its ceiling is not high enough, and T-'s archaic lighting techniques do not help. The only way we can supply their clients with a useable image is by the darkroom staff, G- and K-, manipulating exposures on practically every print to restore a normal range of tones. Not only does T- light his subjects poorly, (and the same way every time,) but instead of checking exposure and composition the modern way (with a polaroid test shot – ready to view in 30 seconds), he exposes a sheet of large format black and white film, which then has to be processed in the dark room. This takes around 15 minutes if done fast, and has to be viewed, still wet, as a negative image for us to gauge any adjustments necessary! The first time he shows me this method, I am too astonished to speak. It's paleolithic! When I do eventually ask about Polaroid, he dismisses it as an unnecessary expense. I must do it his way.

Sadly, the house shooting technique is not the only problem to reveal itself. The camera equipment and lighting itself is almost all about twenty – if not thirty – years out of date, and subsequently slower, less flexible in use, and of low image

History of a Daft A'porth

quality. My six short months spent at D- photography were at least graced with up-to-date equipment and methods, and a creative and skilled approach. The professional set-up here, along with the lack of investment is a huge blow.

Personally, life is also dealing me a rough hand. Viv and I have come to a turning point. Being apart (she in Nottingham, me in London) has added a further wobble to a relationship which was already faltering. Finally, she announces that she can't carry on. We're officially no longer a couple.

Although I half expected it, I'm broken up by the news. It hits me hard, and it'll be months before I fully pull myself back together emotionally.

As if this weren't enough, I discover when my first London winter blows in, that the place I work is not even adequately heated! The studio space has some small electric radiators that just about raise the temperature to a bearable level if you're working hard (ie moving furniture.) The office, however is like something out of Dickens. There are two small chimney-like gas heaters about fifteen cm square and a metre high, equally spaced in a room approximately eight metres by three. The heat they put out wouldn't melt a pat of butter in close contact, and any time passed in the office must be spent wrapped in outdoor clothes, huddled over one of these heaters. The colour darkroom is the warmest place in the building, as the developing and printing machines run at a relatively high temperature. The person I feel sorriest for is K-, our black and white darkroom technician. His workspace could be used as a commercial food chiller. He has one small fan heater, and has to wear several pullovers beneath his white lab coat. Our black and white prints are hand processed in trays of chemicals, and washed in a large sink. His fingers are almost constantly wet, and consequently blue with cold. The whole company is run on the most threadbare of budgets, with not the slightest hint of any desire to improve the work, the assets, or the conditions. When I speak to other photographers I meet, out on a press job or elsewhere, I can't bring myself to truthfully describe where I work. I wouldn't be surprised to see inkwells and quills on J-'s desk, and for T to march in wearing a stovepipe hat.

One saving grace is that at least they allow me to bring Frodo along. He either lies around the office or studio, or goes out for one of his walks, barking to be let back in. As usual, his easy-going character ensures that all, J- and T- included, become quite fond of him. And it's whilst accompanying me here that he achieves his most extraordinary feat to date.

Every day, after breakfast and a brief stroll on his own outside, he comes with me to work in the car. We share a flat in Hornsey, north London, with a friend, John Clifford, whom I knew in Sheffield, and who moved down here a year ago. Frodo curls up on the back seat of the car, and I drive from Hornsey, across ten miles of the north east part of the city, through the busy boroughs of Harringay, Tottenham Hale, Higham Hill, and Walthamstow. We spend the day at work, and he comes home with me in the car. One day, after about a year of this, he's late getting back from his morning trot about. I *have* to get to work on time that day, there's a client coming in. Frodo's been late before. I have to decide. I shrug mentally; he'll have to be outside till I get home (Yes, I know! But things were different then!). So I set off for work. The usual thirty minutes' drive later, I arrive and start work. An hour or so afterwards, we're all in the office when there's a bark at the door.

J- lets him in, and I stare in disbelief at the dog.

"I didn't see him come in with you," says T-

"Er... no... He didn't," I gasp.

"So how did he get here?"

"He must have walked."

"Blimey!"

"How did he know...?"

"I've no idea...!" I reply, equally stunned.

Completely unperturbed by his ten-mile trek from home to office through speeding London rush-hour traffic, along a route he has only ever previously covered in the back of my car, Frodo ambles to his corner and curls up for a nap.

History of a Daft A'porth

Another winter arrives, and we sit like refuseniks in a gulag, mufflered and crouched near the pathetic 'heaters.' If it weren't so tragic, it would be funny. In reality, it's depressing. Driving in to work one day, I hear the tragic news on the radio that John Lennon has been shot and killed in New York. Six months earlier my mother told me that Alice had passed away in hospital. I wondered agonisingly at the time if there might be something wrong with me, as I didn't feel an overwhelming grief. I didn't break down; I didn't cry. It's all the more astonishing, therefore, that on hearing the news of Lennon's assassination, I burst into tears, and have to pull the car over until I recover. Perhaps this man, who wanted so much for us all to love each other, represents a significant and happy part of my past, and how things had changed since my distressing childhood. Although she was part of my salvation, maybe Alice was still so much a part of that traumatic period, that any grief was subsumed by my flight from the painful recollections of that time. Now, hearing of Lennon's death, and filled with the despair born of the oppressive emptiness of my working situation, it seems to me as if optimism itself has been destroyed by Mark Chapman's bullets.

It takes time and persistence, but I eventually persuade T- to let me use Polaroid, and to let me adopt more sophisticated lighting in the studio. Because of this progress, we now build some proper room-sets, and use models in life-style situations (Frodo stars in one kitchen shoot!) We're also picking up more small-product photography, which I love, and in which T has little experience. Even my brief tutelage from Andy at D- Photography brought my skills along far beyond his in this area. Despite the inhibiting conditions, I also manage – shooting extra-curricular images in my own time, to get together enough of a portfolio to apply for a professional qualification...
At the beginning of my employment here, I joined the Master Photographers Association, one of the major professional bodies, as an ordinary non-qualified member. To gain the title of Associate, one has to submit a portfolio of work to be assessed

by a panel one's peers; a minimum of twenty shots showing competence and creativity in a range of subjects and techniques. Working in an environment that's devoid of creative satisfaction, and so appallingly dull and old fashioned, it's vital to me, personally and professionally, to earn the approval of those of my fellow practitioners whose work I respect and admire. I submit my portfolio, and sit through three agonising days awaiting the verdict.

I'm an AMPA!

Much good it does me! Despite formal congratulations from J-, T-, and the others, it does not result in either a pay rise or any improvement in working conditions. K-, the young printer, and I, commiserate and fulminate to each other in secret in his darkroom, over lunch in the local caff', or in the pub after work. Maniacally, we imagine burning the place down, and what could be done to rebuild it properly with the insurance money. We speculate how long we'll be able to stick it out, and how we might persuade the partners to modernise. Or shoot themselves. These are the early 1980's: we're in a recession, unemployment is high, and threatening to resign is unfortunately not a weapon we have in our arsenal.

In the end, foolishly, I orchestrate my own demise.

I am so utterly fed up with the depressing conditions, the low standards, the managerial lethargy, and the lack of any kind of career progress, that I start looking for other work. Photography jobs are like hen's teeth, I've discovered. The monthly British Journal of Photography is the place to look, but there are only about three anywhere near appropriate jobs in each issue, most of them requiring either far more experience than I have, or a particularly esoteric technical specialism. The only other option is to go out on my own. Despite now possessing a small amount of my own professional kit, I've nothing like the means or the space to start my own photography business. It would also require a huge loan, and I have no collateral – I live in a shared rented flat, and I've no savings to speak of. I also have a very small potential client base. I have to try to build something from scratch.

History of a Daft A'porth

The only way I can do this is to carry out work on my own behalf in my spare time. One, albeit small, source of this comes through John, my flatmate. He's a lecturer in lighting and sound at Mountview Theatre School, a few minutes' walk from our flat. Not knowing anyone else in London when I first moved here, I piggy-backed on John's social life, and part of this was the tiny but lively student bar at Mountview. Looking at the front-of-house show photographs displayed in the bar, it's strikingly apparent that they have no animation or real atmosphere of the plays to which they're supposed to attract thrilled audiences. Static, and rigidly posed, they're uniform, flat, and sterile. I approach the principal with an offer. I will take pictures of the next show for free. If I improve significantly on what they have, would he consider my replacing his current photographer? He's hesitant, but, swayed by my careful repetition of the word 'free,' he accepts the bid.

Traditionally, theatre photography *had* to be posed and static; slow films and low illumination levels dictated this approach, and even with new faster films and better cameras, many practitioners are still hidebound by the old habits – as clearly demonstrated at Mountview. My experience as an actor/director, taking front-of-house photos for Theatre Group at university, and the wealth of creative influences I've absorbed studying the work of great photographers, allows me to pursue my own style. Instead of posing the actors in the old way, and using the dead flat light of on-camera flash, I ask the director to set the show lighting for a particularly animated scene, and to have the actors run through it while I move around and sometimes amongst them, capturing them in mid phrase or gesture. We do this for a dozen or so vivid moments in the play, and I speed off to process a set of prints for the following day.

"My goodness me, I'd no idea they could be as good as this!" The school's principal. "and so quick!" My gamble's paid off. I'm hired.

I will take front-of house pictures for Mountview for practically every show for many years, as well as portfolio shots for a good few of the students. Over time, some of them will become good friends. One in particular, a mature student by the name of Mike, will tantalisingly almost give me back my career in the theatre, and together we'll launch a major Hollywood star... Of that, more later.

Mountview, in the meantime, despite my photographing every show, selling reprints to cast members, and taking *Spotlight* head-shots for some of them, creates nowhere near enough revenue to run a full-time business. I investigate expanding my show-photo service into the West End, but that's as firmly sewn up as a Sunday joint, and I have to look elsewhere to build my assets. The only option left to me is to do work 'on the side' using the firm's equipment. This is not something I undertake lightly. It's a big risk, and it's pretty unethical. I justify it to myself as payback for the unacceptable attitudes and conditions under which I have to work. I feel strongly that the physical discomfort, the freezing workspaces, the dire lack – in my eyes – of professionalism, and the seeming indifference to the welfare and progress of their employees, makes it acceptable for me to go behind their backs. It's technically wrong, yes, but both I and K- (in whom I confide, and who occasionally assists me) are so outraged and frustrated by our employers that we endow our rebellion with a kind of Robin Hood character. In this case, we're the poor who benefit!

Working only on location, and borrowing the firm's kit, I carry out jobs for three or four clients.

And then I make a classic mistake.

T- calls me into the office.

"Please sit down...

It seems you've approached one of our clients hoping to do some work for them that wasn't for this company?"

"Ah..." I gape helplessly. T- names the client.

"He's called me as a friend to inform me of this."

I can only nod helplessly. (He was a friend!?)

"J- and I are extremely disappointed, and really quite angry."

"Yes... I...I'm just so... I really need to supplement my salary, and..."

I trail off, not knowing how to explain.

History of a Daft A'porth

"Well, that's no excuse, and frankly we've no option but to let you go, effective immediately. You'll be paid one month's notice, but we'd prefer you to leave straight away."
I'm shell-shocked. But in a way perhaps I expected it; it was a dangerous game to play, and I messed up. Maybe, deep down, I'm glad it's happened...?
I pack up the few personal items I've got scattered around the place, and leave, Frodo following mournfully at my heels.
So, once again, I find myself out of work. I struggle on with the theatre photos, pick up a little bit of commercial work from a couple of designers I made friends with working for K-Photography, but I'm bringing in so little, I have to sign on. There's only the usual crop of unattainable jobs in the BJP. I dispiritedly apply for some of them, even for darkroom technician posts, but nothing comes of it.
Then, unexpectedly, I get a call from the Agfa rep who supplies film and colour printing paper to my erstwhile employers. He's a friendly chap, and we became quite matey while I was there, having lunch together occasionally in the local greasy spoon. He tells me that another client of his is looking for someone.
"It's probably not what you're looking for, Peter, but it could tide you over, maybe. It's a chap in Muswell Hill called P- G-. He's a pharmacist by profession, runs a chemist's shop, but he's a keen photographer, and he's got a bit of a business above his shop specialising in black and white materials. He's making a name for himself as a supplier, and he needs some more help."
"Mmmm.... retail...."
"Yes... but it's quality stuff. They're on a bit of a crusade to improve people's techniques in black and white. The perfect negative, the perfect print, and all that... at least till you find something else..."
I see the sense in this, I'm grateful, and decide to take a look.
P- G- interviews me in the little office-come-order-room-come-dispatch-area above the pharmacy. His story is that, in despair of the desperate quality of black and white film, printing paper, and processing materials in the UK, he and a colleague, M-, drove a Transit van to Agfa in Germany, loaded as much in as

they could, and drove it back here for their own use and resale to a few aficionados. Word got out; they began ordering more from Agfa; and it took off so precipitously that Agfa decided to begin manufacture of these products again at their London plant. P- , M-, and their employee, N-, now supply top-grade Agfa film, papers, developers, and other chemicals to discerning amateurs, a growing quantity of colleges, and increasing numbers of professional darkrooms nation-wide. They're also becoming the go-to people for advice on – and materials for – archival storage and conservation of negatives and prints, and consequently are also supplying some prestigious museum departments. Drawing on their extensive research and experience, they're putting together a one-hundred-page booklet detailing methods for producing the 'perfect' negative, and from this, the 'perfect 'print, as well as how to tone, dry, finish, and store these in an optimal manner. (Accomplished, of course, with products supplied by P- G-). His own photographs – a small collection of which are on the walls in the office – are excellent. He shows me the booklet. It's a revelation. I thought I was pretty knowledgeable, but once again, I discover how little I know on a subject. The booklet's full of detailed and logical methodology derived from the likes of Edward Weston and Ansell Adams: photographers renowned for both their incredible clarity of vision and the superlative technical quality of their work. Chapters lay out a route map for any photographer using black and white films and paper, to work to the highest possible standards. I'm very impressed. My consequent eagerness to explore these possibilities, along with G's hearty recommendation, get me the post. Incredibly, Frodo's welcome too. He works his magic wherever he goes!

I start my new job. It's oddly exciting... for a sales job. All of us have to spend some fairly servile time on the downstairs photo counter, taking in holiday snaps for processing by one of the big labs, selling assorted photographic goods such as instant cameras, photo albums, and so on, and occasionally helping the pharmacy side of the shop when they're busy. The main part of the job, however, is upstairs in the hive of activity that is the

History of a Daft A'porth

office. There, we answer phone enquiries about materials and methods, and give advice; we take orders, process them, pack and dispatch them, and we compile the printed *Guide* that inspired me at my interview. This little A5 gem is a distillation of the very best methods to achieve ultimate technical quality in black and white. It offers no creative advice, but anyone following its methodology will produce finely tuned negatives and prints of superb and lasting finish. The results obtained using these methods, and the materials recommended, are a universe away from the poorly exposed film and the resulting washed-out, muddy grey prints on cheap paper commonly seen in many portfolios and galleries. Once again, I find myself plunged into an environment in which I must learn an awful lot in a very short time. My own photography benefits enormously. Word of this place and its philosophy spreads, and soon we're entertaining famous names who want the images they make to be processed our way. Fashion photographer Terence Donovan pops in for a coffee and a chat, and orders some printing paper. He's jolly, friendly, business-like. I come back in from lunch one day to see Britain's most famous snapper, David Bailey in my chair, feet up on the desk, cheerfully demanding 'Let's 'ave a gander at this Record Rapid then," (Agfa's premium printing paper), and peppering the ensuing long discussion on method with frequent, good-natured obscenities.

A completely different encounter, however, and one that culminates in a sobering and emotional event, is with Don McCullin, the renowned war photographer. As soon as he walks in, accepts the invitation to take tea, and begins to talk, it's obvious that this man has been through stuff we could not imagine. Polite, quiet, well-spoken and warm, there's an aura about him that's unmistakeably that of buried pain. He never talks directly about the things he's seen, just the practicalities of image-making in his job, but after he's left, we look at each other, and everything unsaid in that quiet chat is left clearly hanging in the air, sombre and sad. Because these world-famous photographers have 'adopted' us,' we're invited to openings of all the exhibitions they have in London. They're all very glossy affairs, but the one that will burn itself indelibly into my memory is that of McCullin's *"Beirut,"* a collection of his pictures of conflict in that city, held at the Olympus Gallery in central London. When we arrive, it's already busy; faces from fashion, photography, and journalism mingle with politicians, actors, and artists. The walls are hung with Don's black and white images printed on forty by thirty cm Record Rapid, selenium-toned to endow the dark areas with a rich, deep purply brown lustre. They are beautifully, luxuriously, printed; almost edibly gorgeous: ultimate proof of the adage that there is no art without craft. As for the content of the pictures... The Lebanese civil war is at its height in the eighties, and the subject matter in these exquisitely finished prints is a relentless and intimate catalogue of the pain, anguish, death, and despair of that war. As a viewer, you're stunned. The juxtaposition one's invited to view is, on the one hand, stunning image-making allied to superb printing, and on the other, a story of heart-rending misery. Paradoxically, the very craftsmanship that has led to the superlative technical quality of these images, amplifies and deepens the misery and despair they portray. One's left floundering in a numbing whirlpool of reactions. The photographs are those of a master journalist, skilfully transferred to paper by a darkroom technician at the top of their game, but if you have any human feelings at all, the subject matter catches your breath, shakes you violently, and grasps at your heart until the tears run down your face. The gallery is filled with stupefied people wandering from print to print, carrying untouched plates of very expensive canapés, and staring, lost, into a dark space far beyond the room and the city in which they find themselves.

Other exhibitions we see are just as beautifully presented, just as carefully and expertly crafted, and portray fascinating and illuminating subjects, but I will never recall any of them as vividly and movingly as I shall recall Don's *"Beirut."*

Alas the P- G- job does not last long. A few months in, and the novelty's worn off. Working in a shop does not have lasting

History of a Daft A'porth

appeal for me. Other mail-order suppliers have latched onto the idea that photographers, amateur and professional alike, want top quality materials, and are making inroads into the field of supply. Ilford are now producing their *Gallery* papers to rival Agfa's range, and supplies of all these materials are becoming more readily available across the UK. The business is also not doing as well as before, and P-'s getting edgy. At last, the moment comes when, regretfully, he says, he can no longer afford to keep me on.

Yet again, I find myself unemployed!

Yet again, however, the guardian angel I inexplicably appear to have looking after my job prospects comes to the rescue. There's an ad in the BJP(at last!) for a catalogue photographer at the Central London headquarters of one of the major auction houses.

At the interview, N-, my potential boss, explains that their photography is currently bought-in. A commissioned photographer visits once a week to take shots of all items for that week's sale catalogue. The new post-holder would be responsible for setting up and managing an in-house department to replace this service. A darkroom will be built to their specifications to facilitate black and white film and print processing.

He's impressed with my portfolio, and after a tough grilling to determine my management capabilities, he offers me the job. That was easy...?

I seem to have a habit of getting myself employed by businesses that don't turn out as expected. My own fault for not doing the research. In this case, it doesn't take long to become evident.

Whilst I supervise the conversion of a backroom in the firm's West London premises into a B/W darkroom, the external photographer continues – with poorly disguised ill grace – to make his weekly visits. This continues for some weeks, but eventually it's down to me. I had formed the impression during the interview that I would have a proper studio space and equipment, but instead find myself consigned to a cramped and dusty corner of 19th Century pictures storage in the basement area of the central London auction house. I have at least persuaded N- to buy a new Sinar large-format studio camera, tripod, and lighting, but the working area is dreadful! The basement has a two-storey stack for the paintings that takes up three quarters of the space; I'm crammed into the remaining dusty quarter. Every week, I receive from the various departments, porcelain, clocks and watches, fabrics, silverware, paintings, etc, all the items destined for the next sale. I have a large table and some glass shelves on which to display them, singly or grouped, and a white background. There's a separate space at the Fulham premises, where furniture and other large items are auctioned. After each central shoot, I take the film on the bus, to the darkroom, process that and the furniture shots, and make prints of the hundred or so items. These I then distribute to the heads of department for approval and eventual dispatch to the catalogue printers.

Intrinsically, the objects are fascinating. Some are exceptionally valuable. Many are beautiful – I learn to particularly adore Lalique glassware – but others are so plain, or so patently ugly, one wonders why anyone would ever wish to own them. Notwithstanding their variety or qualities, it requires little or no creativity to transfer them to film. It's necessary only to possess enough lighting skill to record them in accurate detail for potential buyers to evaluate them in the catalogue. Nonetheless, even this basic level of competence merits a decent work-space, but despite my repeated requests for a real studio, I'm told I must continue where I am "for the time being." At least, unlike at K- Photography, I'm not freezing!

Precious and pretty antiques or not, it doesn't take long before this work too becomes tedious. After a few run-ins with department heads used to the previous photographer's (to my mind, wishy-washy) prints, I'm producing results they all agree are an improvement, and I've even become quite pally with a couple of them. Time to push a little.

The weekly auction catalogue, an A5 booklet, is a dreary affair, with a single cut-out objet-d'art, painting, or furniture item on

History of a Daft A'porth

its cover. If the item is of particular interest, it's shot in colour, but still on a plain ground. I'm convinced they're missing a trick here. The catalogue is a major part of marketing, and they're not making the most of its potential.

So, one day, presented with a huge and very expensive oriental vase to shoot, I decide to move things along a little. I get in some sand and a couple of palm leaves, spray-paint some white clouds on a sky-blue background, and shoot the vase in colour on a 'desert island' set with 'tropical sun' lighting. The following day, having received the processed film back from the lab, I present the result to F-, the young, trendy, open-minded head of porcelain, with whom I'm on good terms. Explaining my theory, I suggest the image as a cover for the catalogue. F- is impressed and encouragingly enthusiastic about the idea.

It has to pass senior management, however, and they're not known for their thrusting modernity. I discover later from F- that there's been heated debate. The company is an old established family business, and their resistance to change is legendary. As usual, the older directors wish to keep things just as they've always been (I feel like I've been here before). Luckily two things help to tip the balance; there are sufficient younger managers who feel the need to update, and I've deliberately captured the vase in a way that's sufficiently different and intriguing, but not so outrageous that they find it 'revolutionary'.

It goes on the cover.

The effect is startling, even to me. They sell around fifty percent more catalogues, and subsequent auction sales reflect this. I've been more than justified by the good old bottom line. I'm officially asked to produce a 'creative' cover shot every week from now on. In the coming months, I manage to push the boundaries a little further, using soft focus, overlapping objects, close-up partial sections, and lots of carefully matched atmospheric props. When the firm is asked to handle the sale of the contents of a stately home in Derbyshire, I'm aided by glorious weather to shoot a front cover of the stunning Elizabethan house set in its grounds. It sells like hot cakes!

Frodo, of course, is not permitted here. John and I have had had to move out; the landlord is selling up. Earning a reasonable, if far from luxurious salary, I can afford a place of my own. Well, almost... I've found a first-floor flat not far away, in Harringay. I sublet a room to a Mountview theatre school tech student called Barney. Our landlords are a Greek family who run the cassette-tape shop on the ground floor. In the flat above is a chap called Phil. The Greek family is brilliant. We're soon the best of friends, and they love Frodo. If Barney's not there, they're happy to let the dog in and out of the street door up to my flat whenever he barks, and he's usually waiting on the landing for me when I come home. Occasionally, Phil will look after him, and take him to the park. It's a nice flat, with a window overlooking the Harringay dog-track, where, on a fine Saturday afternoon, perched astride my window ledge, I can listen to music through my massive pair of headphones, and watch the dogs careering round in ferocious pursuit of a stuffed bunny. It would be nice to have both the two main rooms, but I'm not earning quite enough. Hence Barney. Had I not had to share, I wouldn't experience what must be one of the silliest and most embarrassing moments of my life...

I'm still taking photographs for Mountview, but haven't had time yet to arrange a full darkroom blackout in my bedroom, which has two massive windows. Printing paper is a little more forgiving of incomplete blackout, but film requires total darkness. One Saturday, I find myself with a Mountview show film that needs urgent processing. To do this I must transfer it from its cassette into a light-tight processing container, a plastic screw-top cylinder. It's a bright summer's day, and there's nowhere in the flat dark enough. I try under the bed clothes... no: surprisingly light. Where? There's only one place in the whole flat that comes to mind... Barney's wardrobe. Mine's too small. He's out. I have no idea when he'll be back. Shall I risk it? I do. I go into his room, and climb into the wardrobe with the film and the cylinder. In the dark, I snap open the cassette, and start to entwine the film onto the plastic spiral that will hold it

History of a Daft A'porth

in its developing tank. This will only take me about forty-five seconds, and I'll be out.

Inevitably, Barney comes back. I hear him enter his room, and start moving around, humming cheerfully.

Three things can happen:

1. He leaves without discovering me.
2. He opens his wardrobe and finds me hiding in it.
3. I tell him I'm in his wardrobe.

(3a. Why on earth didn't I think to leave him a note outside the door!?)

Number one would of course be the desired winner, but how long could I endure waiting for it? Of the remaining runners, number three limps into first place as the least unbearable option. I take a deep breath...

"Barney, I know this is weird, but please don't worry..."

"What the ...?"

"I'm in your wardrobe."

"...!..."

"It's the only place dark enough to load a film, and it was urgent. I was a bit desperate... I'm really sorry!"

"... O....K...."

The film is safely loaded. I push open the door, and extract myself from the interior of the wardrobe. Barney has the kind of look on his face you would expect from someone who has just found his flat-mate in his wardrobe.

I repeat my apologies even more profusely, elaborating on the urgency of the job and my desperation. He's far more forgiving than I have a right to accept; even seems to find it rather amusing: he subsequently revels in telling the story to his friends –especially in my presence. After this day, however, he's never quite as jolly or spontaneous with me as before. There appears to be no animosity, but from now until he moves out a year later, I feel I'm sharing with a less intimate friend.

The management are sufficiently pleased with my work to give me a pay rise. I am also now on much better terms with all the department heads. Initially, despite my title of Photographic

Manager, some of them treated me no better than a servant, ordering me around like one of their long-suffering and much put-upon porters. My efforts having proved profitable to the firm, and having raised the visibility of the items they handle for auction, I'm now accepted as on a par. Well, almost... there'll always be one or two who see their perch as a branch or two up the pecking order from mine. But everyone's now friendly enough. The work, on the other hand, is boring, and I'm still, after two years, in the same cramped and dusty corner of the basement. I've mastered every technique under the sun to get the very best out of silverware, moulded glass, elaborately carved wood, faded oil paintings, etc, and frankly, they're all starting to look the same. My once-a-week foray into creativity is mildly stimulating, but restricted by the lack of subject variety. I'm in a rut. Again. And for a studio photographer, a not-that-well-paid-rut at that. I start looking for another job.

I get one or two interviews, but it's another six months of antiques tedium before I find one that might promise results.
H- Studios is a commercial photography business in West London, specialising in PR and industrial work. With trepidation, I take along my portfolio containing my AMPA pictures, some auction catalogue front cover shots, and a few more elaborate images I've again created for folio use only. I'm interviewed by the business' two photographer-owners, R- and B-.
They're open and friendly, but the questioning is intense. I'm shown the small but well-equipped studio and darkrooms, and they outline the job specifications.
They've three more people to see, and the next few days for me are purgatory.
And then... wow!... I've got the job! (Six months' probation period). A real studio job! A proper studio! (and heated!)
I spend the next few days, during my spare time, writing a three-page report on my reasons for leaving my current employ, with consequent and detailed recommendations for improvements if they wish to attract and keep a replacement of half decent

History of a Daft A'porth

calibre. I present this report, neatly typed, to my boss, along with my resignation,
Much to my satisfaction, and providing not a little irony, they beg me to stay. They offer me a substantial pay rise, *and* a studio. (Horse? Stable? Bolted?). T-, one of the directors, who was especially and stubbornly critical of my efforts at the beginning, personally pleads with me not to quit. I make it politely but firmly plain that nothing they can possibly offer will persuade me to change my mind.
One day, approximately a year in the future, I will pop in to say a brief hello to the friends I made here, only to be shown the lovely custom-built studio space my replacement is using! Ah well...

But here and now it's my first day at H-Studios; at last, I'm a proper photographer working for a proper, modern commercial studio!
After struggling for so long in a kind of professional wilderness, it's the long-awaited kickstart to a career that will last for the next fourteen years, and in which I'll find enormous personal, creative, and professional satisfaction.
The work at H- is exactly what I wished for; small products in the studio, packaged food, jewellery, toys, drinks, tools, kitchenware, and every kind of small consumer item. We also shoot on location, producing prints and transparencies of personnel, offices, factories, machinery, and outdoor settings. It's enormously varied work, involving close collaboration with the clients, and bizarrely exactly parallels my very first photographic job in Sheffield – without the having to sell pop-up booths!
My background in theatre serves me well: people skills comprising a fundamental part of the job, and I quickly establish easy working relationships with the clients. All the hard work I put into my previous jobs to increase their creative content also pays off. Most of the clients allow us complete creative licence for setting their products, using a range of 'table-tops,' backgrounds, and props. Some budgets are small, sometimes

very small, and then we use props from a stock range in the studio, but when there's more cash to splash, we buy in props, and small shopping expeditions are a part of the routine. I start by shadowing B- in the studio, and R- on location, but they eventually see I'm capable, and I'm let off the leash. I'm a little apprehensive when the six-month period is up, but learn that I've fulfilled my probation criteria. I become officially one of the team. My salary, though still not huge, is better, and there's also a car allowance. This all means that when Barney graduates and moves out, I can now afford the flat on my own.

Barney's room becomes my bedroom, and mine the living room. I've my own place! I'm a grown-up! The job's going well. I've a wide circle of friends in the area, thanks once again to my pal John Clifford: we all drink in the local pubs, go to gigs, play cricket, and hold wild parties. London is now well and truly my home, and I love it.

How London will surprise me, though, is that as well as furnishing me with a new career and new friends, it will open up two other separate worlds for me; worlds I've previously only tentatively explored, and which one would never think to associate with one of the largest, most metropolitan cities in the world. And yes, once more, I owe both, indirectly but inevitably, to the indispensable and ubiquitous John.

History of a Daft A'porth

Chapter 13:   Dance the night away

It's the heart afraid of breaking that never learns to dance.
Xiaolu Guo

Shortly after moving from Sheffield to London in 1980, and sharing both a flat, *and* a social life with John, I'm easily persuaded by him, one sunny June day, to drive to his home town of Stroud for his birthday party, taking along a bunch of our London mates in my car. When we arrive, the party's in full swing – in a field! There are tables laden with the usual food and drink, there are people standing chatting; but there's also an antique farm cart with a folk band on it, and several people in a group obviously waiting to start a dance of some kind. As my friends and I pile out of the car, we're surprised but delighted to have descend upon us an equivalent number of pretty girls, who drag us onto the 'dance floor,' i.e. the field. After what I later find out is 'the caller' has given us instructions as to how the dance should go, the band strikes up, and we're off!
My last experience of ceilidh dancing was sitting grumpily with a pint in the corner of a university hall while the friends who had persuaded me to come got on with having fun. Right from the start at John's birthday party, no-one is allowed to sit out. And I'm astonished by the thrill and the joy that suddenly grabs me – just as our dance partners have, and continue to. It's another 'apple pie moment!' What have I been missing all these years? This is so much fun! And these girls! You ask a girl to dance, and unless exhausted by the dance, or nursing a broken leg, she'll never say no! It's totally removed from the Russian roulette of humiliation that is your average disco.
This afternoon of wildness converts me utterly, and on our return to London, I become a regular attendee at ceilidhs in the city (where I discover there's a thriving scene), and at folk festivals. Although there's a huge range of ages, most of the dancers are around my own, and thanks to a ceilidh at Cecil Sharpe House, the London-based centre for English Folk Music,

I will meet my second long-term girlfriend, but we'll come to that in a bit.

The high point of all this madness is Sidmouth. In full, the Sidmouth International Folk Festival. This is one of, if not *the* largest festival of folk music and dance in Europe. Brought up with the traditions in the Cotswold town of Stroud, my mate John has been going to the Sidmouth Festival for years. After the joy and fizz of his birthday party, I take little persuading to buy a ticket for the whole week, camping included. The festival, which an estimated one hundred thousand people visit over the seven days, is held every August in the tiny Devon resort. Performers, participants, and spectators descend on the town from all over the world. A large open-air arena, seating several hundred people, is built every year on the outskirts of the town, and hosts displays of traditional music and dance from dozens of visiting British and foreign groups. These range from traditional English Morris 'sides,' through eastern European circle dances, African village close-harmony chanting dance, to Chinese lion dances and Appalachian square. Over the course of the festival's many years, almost every country in the world has sent dancers and/or singers to Sidmouth.

As well as performing in the arena, the dancers spend a large part of their time running workshops in smaller venues or at some of the other major events. At these workshops, any who wish – accomplished dancers or not – can learn the basic steps and rhythms of the particular country's traditions. These are a source of huge joy for me: the enthusiasm of the dancers, the incredible variety of step patterns and group formations, the laughter as we get them hopelessly wrong, and the wide smiles and spontaneous applause when we finally master a few simple steps. It's heart-warming. If we do well, the class may even be invited to give a little exhibition of what we've learned, during breaks at some of the big ceilidhs.

There are singers' and musicians' workshops all over the town as well. Every pub, every schoolroom, every weather-tight shed, has been commandeered. Add to this the multitude of performances

History of a Daft A'porth

– programmed or spontaneous – taking place on the streets and promenade, and walking through the town becomes a stroll from tune to tune, from fiddle to clarinet, from sea shanty to brass band. It's a chaotic, yet melodic cornucopia of sound and movement.

Because John's a regular here, he knows quite a few other veterans, and some of the performers. He and his friends – many from Stroud or nearby – arrange to camp together, and I'm invited to join the hallowed ranks.

It really is something else. Over the years, John and the others have refined and perfected the art of Sidmouth camping. The only official provisions made on the site are toilets. Everything else is up to you. If you want a shower, the town rugby club offers theirs for a small fee. But they're often busy, and it's a pain going into town just for a wash. It's either an extra twenty-minute walk there and back, or an impossible search for a parking spot. So, John and co have set up their own. He brings a petrol-powered pump and heater, an enormous water tank, a shower head with hose, and a contrivance of sticks and canvas for a cubicle. Hot showers for the lucky group members! And not only ablutions: alongside the shower is the cook-tent, complete with full-size four-ring kitchen gas-cooker with oven, a trestle table, and a big sink with another water tank and heater.

We take it in turns to cook a full sit-down meal every evening for around a dozen people, with a rota for washing-up.

Just to complete this picture of domestic bliss, the second year I attend, John turns up with half a dozen whitewashed edging stones, an equal number of potted plants, and two garishly coloured gnomes, with which we proceed to establish our 'front garden.' Such a wonder is our corner of the campsite, that it becomes a visitor attraction in itself.

My absolute favourite moments here, though, are spent in the ceilidhs.

There are some afternoon dances calling themselves ceilidhs, that are a little staid, but where you can pick up some interesting dance skills or etiquette, and to which I occasionally go, but it's the Drill Hall Ceilidh at 8pm, and the Late Night Extra afterwards, in a huge marquee on the edge of town, that are the unmissable events of every evening. Unmissable for the hard core, that is. And I now count myself amongst this dedicated band. Over the months since John's birthday, and in my first few forays into the festival, I find I've an unexpected gift for what is rather formally known as 'Social Dance.' This definition covers all dances you do with other people; couple dances, set dances, square dances and circle dances. Just like electrons in motion around an atomic nucleus, these can vary enormously in energy level and space required, sometimes, but not always, depending on age and fitness. The level of vigour ranges widely, from a sedate walk of the circles, forwards and backs, do-si-do's, stars etc, in gentle rhythm with the music, all the way to wild and boisterous commitment to the irresistibly accelerating weaving patterns: hand over hand, in and out, round and round, whirling around each other, spinning at impossible speeds, elbow locked in your partner's. It sounds utterly out of control, but there's a sensibility – an awareness of the presence of the other dancers, a feel for the space around you, however wild the jig, the reel or the hop-step. Inconsiderate dancers, who allow their abandon to the energy of the dance to impinge painfully on others, are frowned upon, and (usually gently) castigated. Crazy is allowed, but not that crazy!

The Drill Hall is a dilapidated but comfortable shed-like structure on the sea front, that normally welcomes meetings of the local scout troop. It holds about fifty or sixty people comfortably spaced. Around twice that cram in there for the ceilidhs. These are legendary, and culminate in the madness that is the End-of-Festival Fancy-Dress Ceilidh. I revel in the eccentric eclecticism of variously: a Rocky Horror ceilidh, a Zombies ceilidh, a Renaissance ceilidh, a Vicars and Tarts ceilidh, and other such flights of imagination. Memorable above all, is a Rock and Roll ceilidh, for the start of which the band's caller is noisily and majestically driven from the street to the stage on the back of a growling Harley Davidson.

Each of the incredible bands manage to create a cross-over musical genre, blending whatever is the theme of the night with

History of a Daft A'porth

high energy English folk-dance tunes. It's always wild, always packed, always sweaty. So much so, that I take to permanently carrying a towel stuffed through my belt, and storing a spare T-shirt in the car for the trip up to the Late Night Extra.

For my Sidmouth group of friends, the Late-Night Extra is the one event that *cannot* be missed. It starts at eleven, and goes on till two or sometimes three in the morning. It's like a version of the Drill Hall magnified twenty times. A massive tent, wooden-floored, and a maelstrom of line upon line, or circle after circle, of riotously happy dancers weaving frenetically but skilfully in and out with each other to the pulsing rhythms of electric folk, and the jolly, at times hilariously caustic, interjections of the caller. He or she, ever watchful for the chaos of a group who can't remember the instructions for the dance, and are helplessly milling about, will suddenly launch themselves through the melee of the dance, thread their way to the ailing group with the agility of a scrum half dodging the opposing team, sort them out with encouraging shouts and shoves in the right directions, then speed back to the stage to miraculously pick up calling at precisely the right point.

There are no wallflowers here. No-one is left out. When a dance is preparing its lines, sets, or circles, ready to start, there are always gaps to fill. Anyone stood or sat around the edge – exhausted or not, will be cajoled, begged, pleaded with to make up a set and fill the voids so the dance can start. Callers are merciless in their persuasion, and will occasionally fill in a gap themselves if the mood takes them and they feel we can manage without their directions. I throw myself into almost every dance throughout the evening, taking a rare break now and again to replenish my beer glass, or go to the loo. My belt towels serve me well over the many festivals I attend, becoming a recognised trade mark.

The end of the Late-Night Extra is always marked by a Polka, played by the band as the tired but joyful guests leave the tent for their various accommodations, and to which the most dedicated and energetic dancers commit themselves, enjoying the space generated as most of the others leave. This smaller band – me included – make the most of the floor, carouselling at breakneck speed around the tent to the frenetic two by two skip-step of the Polka. We keep this up until the very last notes, when the music reaches its final climax, and dies. At which, we say our thank-you's and goodbyes to the band, and exit, steaming, into the starry night – to wend our way to wherever we sleep.

The festival falls during the same season as the Perseid meteor shower, and sometimes, having arrived back at the tents ready for a last cuppa or a snifter, we pass the final hours after all the noise and celebration leaning sleepily back in our camp chairs, silently watching the heavens in the hope catching the fleeting, incandescent streak of a dying celestial visitor. I'm blessed to see several over the years.

The following day, we're up and ready to do it all again!

I'm accompanied at the festival, of course, by my trusty four-legged companion. He goes with me to many of the smaller events in pubs and halls, but seems quite content to spend an hour or two in the car (window cracked open of course) if he's not allowed in somewhere. Most of the day, we're both out and about in the town, dropping in to a dance, a music or poetry event here and there, meeting friends, or paddling in the sea (One year, a group of us execute a complete Cornish Four-Hand-Reel up to our knees in the sea – not an easy feat – to the cheers of onlookers).

Frodo sports his own set of Morris bells presented to him by a friend who dances with a Gloucester side. As we're strolling along the esplanade one day, enjoying the sun and the impromptu performers, the BBC news team covering the festival spots him loping along behind me, his bells jingling. A brief negotiation takes place, and subsequently, that evening he makes a brief but much celebrated appearance on the BBC News footage of the festival; trotting along; the cameraman tracking him backwards; Frodo gazing enigmatically into the lens. Fame!

Back in London, I start going to the ceilidhs at Cecil Sharp House. They're a pale copy of the Drill Hall knees-ups, but nonetheless, usually energetic and fun. The usual rules apply:

History of a Daft A'porth

care and consideration for the other dancers, and never refuse an invitation to dance without very good reason!

Different people have different approaches to dancing. Some follow the rhythm in a staid, almost academic manner, stepping out the figures as though walking to the music. Another group have a lighter, child-like skip, tripping through the figures as though circling the Maypole at a village fête. A final set – in which I include myself – abandon themselves completely to the pace of the music, bouncing around in a manner more akin to the livelier Morris sides, and – within the bounds of considerate care for the other dancers – leaping and spinning like spring lambs at the more energetic points of the dance. This is the kind of partner with whom I prefer to dance. Not for me the walkers or skippers if there are leapers and spinners to join!

And so it is on one Saturday evening as I walk into one of the Cecil Sharpe 'Knees-Ups.' As soon as I arrive at the already under-way event, I spot a girl dancing who obviously fits into this final group. She's throwing herself around in a joyfully wild, but confidently skilful way, at the far end of the room, and the only one there who seems to be enjoying herself that much. As soon as that dance is over, and another one begins setting up, I invite her onto the floor. I like to ask at the start if I may know who I'm dancing with. This little scrap of intimacy shared by swapping names makes it a lot easier to ask someone to dance again, and has facilitated some friendships that, without names, might never have flourished. She's called Cherry. We have a great first dance, and I ask if she'd like to stay on the floor for the next. She does, and we chat a little before it starts. She lives in Ealing, and works for a major retailer in London as a marketing executive. Etiquette demands that I don't monopolise her on the dance floor, and because she's such a good dancer, she's a popular choice of partner, but I manage to grab her again later. This time, it's she who asks me to stay for the succeeding dance. A good sign! We partner up for the rest of the ceilidh. I've come here today with – guess who... John. At the end of the ceilidh, it being a Saturday night, he invites people back to his place for a couple or three beers. To my delight and surprise, Cherry agrees to accompany me there.

It's the start of a five-year relationship.

The beginning is wonderful, of course. I sometimes stay at her place in Ealing, which is not a long drive from my work, and occasionally she stays at mine in Harringay. Sadly, I no longer have to consider the problem of looking after Frodo. I've lost my great friend: Frodo is no longer with me. He disappeared from my life some months ago, and I'm still grieving his loss. We were together for thirteen years, and he was far, far more than just a canine companion, he was a true soulmate. He is deeply and achingly missed. I will never have another dog.

Sad though it is, it does mean that I can stay across town. But for Cherry and me, as with many couples in the same situation, it becomes a chore to flit between properties, and as our relationship is settling and solidifying, we take the leap to move in together. Her Ealing flat is too small, so she sells up, and we buy a one-bedroom garden flat in trendy Crouch End. It has a to-die-for view from the kitchen across to Alexandra Palace on the other side of the valley, with its iconic radio mast. We have a cheery neighbour – Chris – in the flat above; and another, we eventually discover: a man on the top floor with obvious mental problems. This poor disturbed soul later becomes more frightening and erratic, slamming doors, shouting, and throwing the dustbins around in unexplained fury. On one occasion we call the police. Coming back down from the flat, having managed to calm the occupant, the attending officer shakes his head with dismay, telling us that the top floor is stuffed to the gunnels with hoarded magazines and boxes; the chap is obviously mentally ill. After this we tread much more carefully, avoiding any action that could be construed as confrontational, and thankfully things return to a quiet state. One unexpected but happy consequence of this upset, is that we get to know Chris a lot better, and he becomes a close friend. So much so, that decades later, my family and I will visit him and his adorable wife Eva in their lovingly restored villa in the Tuscan mountains, to which they move permanently in the nineties.

History of a Daft A'porth

Cherry and I make a home together in the flat, decorating, buying furniture, gardening etc, and of course we take holidays together. She too is a keen walker, and the Lake District features high on her list of favourite places. Despite her family and background in Northern Ireland, we never visit. It's to the lakes that we go.

And it's in the lakes that we have a traumatic, miraculous, narrow escape from violent death.

It's the end of our stay, and we're on the way home. This being the Lake District, it's pouring with rain, and has been doing so for days. We've come up here with some London friends, who are some miles behind us in another vehicle, and we've arranged a coffee-break at Ambleside. Cherry and I are in her company car, a top of the range mini, and it's my turn at the wheel. We're following the A591, the main road that snakes north-south through the lakes. This section is wide, without the sharp curves and high walls of the northern stretches, and is well maintained. As we crest a small rise and begin to descend a straight, sloping section with hills to our left and a sharply falling valley on the right, I notice that the road ahead looks particularly wet. Not just rainfall wet, but actually submerged. We're doing around fifty miles an hour, perfectly safe for a good road, even in the rain, but this sight prompts me to decelerate abruptly.

As I hit the brakes, we run into what turns out to be deep water cascading from the hills and pouring across the road. It's so deep that the tyres lose all traction, and the car begins to aquaplane. It's at this point that the stories of everything going into slow motion in such moments reveal themselves to be true. I've read that psychologists and neurologists believe the brain 'speeds up' in some way, the processes of cognition going into overdrive so as to better calculate the actions necessary to preserve the body. And it happens now; exactly like that. The whole world seems to slow to a crawl, like a film projector that's been switched to a lower frame-rate. In this soupy time space, I take my foot off the brake, and apply what I dredge from my memory as the correct 'cadence braking' procedure: tapping the pedal rapidly

with my toe to try and regain some traction. I can't, the water is too deep; we're effectively afloat, drifting gradually across to the opposite side and into the path of an oncoming vehicle. Trying to steer the car back to the left has no effect apart from edging its back end even further to the right. On our right-hand side, we're approaching the high kerb up to a grassy verge overlooking the valley below. Ahead, now only yards away, is the oncoming car, its driver's petrified expression clearly visible, and which despite his own braking, and because of the water, we're approaching at undiminished speed. The only choice I have left is to *encourage* the car's drift to the right, and try to bump it up onto the verge out of the path of the other vehicle. As I turn the wheel that way, and we meet the kerb, the car reacts by abruptly and fiercely mounting it, violently jerking the steering wheel from my grasp, and flinging itself and us out into space over the precipitous valley below. Grass, rock and the stream revolve through our field of view as the car plummets, somersaulting, into the void. It hits the ground on its roof – the compression causing all the windows to pop out with a loud whump – rebounds, turning completely over to bounce again on its nose. I reach for Cherry's hand, and call her name in blind panic. I know we are going to die here. We bounce again with a low grunting crash, roll once more, and come suddenly to rest the right way up.
There's silence.
Silence apart from the sound of rushing water. I look across to Cherry. She's staring at me with the same uncomprehending look. We're still alive! Not only that, but apart from seatbelt burns and a bruise on my shin from the underside of the dashboard, we're unharmed! We open the doors and exit the car – only to slip helplessly chest-deep into the freezing cold river into which the car has plunged. Amazingly it's come to a halt balanced on rocks in the middle of this torrent. We're both torn away from the car by the force of the flood, and swept downstream. Are we to escape a horrendous crash, only to be drowned in the floodwater? Providentially, we both wash up against rocks in slightly shallower water, and manage to cling on. Above us, what seems miles away on the road, vehicles have

History of a Daft A'porth

pulled up. From one of them, a white van, half a dozen people are streaming down the slope towards us. I must be hallucinating – they're all wearing wetsuits! Quickly reaching the swollen river, they plunge in, prise us like limpets from the rock, and haul us out of the freezing water on to the bank. After checking for injury, they wrap us in blankets and half walk, half carry us up and into their van, in which they drive us to the nearest hospital, in Ambleside.

It transpires they were a canoeing club: hence the attire.

Returning to the scene later with our friends, after medical checks, and giving a statement to the police, we try to describe the event (which they blithely drove past a few minutes after the accident). They scoff at the idea that we've survived a plunge thirty feet into a ravine. We arrive at the scene to find the poor mini, as claimed, thirty feet below, amongst huge boulders we had also somehow avoided. Its nose is concertinaed, the wheels are splayed at right-angles in a crazy automotive version of the splits, the windows form an exploded diagram halfway down the hill, and luggage is strewn along its flight path. It had even bounced over a fence into the stream. Our companions are suitably speechless.

We discover later that this is an infamous accident black spot. Just an hour after us, a small van went off the same road into the same river half a mile further along. Miraculously the driver walked away from that too!

A year later they put up a crash barrier.

I discover that Cherry can sing. And she has a beautiful voice. Clear and soft, it reminds me of the late and much missed Sandy Denny. So reminiscent is it, that when she accedes to my pleas, and sings Denny's gently lyrical *Crazy Man Michael*, or the desperately haunting *Who Knows Where the Time Goes*, I'm moved to tears. Sandy was one of my musical gods. Death is always tragic, whoever it may take. The philosopher John Donne, famous for the words '*No man is an island*," wrote in the same poem, "*Any man's death diminishes me*," and the death of someone we revere can move us sometimes as much as a that of a close friend or family member. As witnessed by my reaction to John Lennon's assassination. Sandy Denny died from a ridiculous accident, and joined the ranks of fallen musical heroes, Lennon, Hendrix, Moon, Morrison, et al, all lost through some tragic misadventure.

Alongside idols from other veins of our lives – for me, the Kennedys, Gandhi, Martin Luther King, Alec Guinness, Stephen Hawking, and so many, many others – these brief visitors form milestones along the path of our lives, and leaving them behind can provoke deep feelings of grief and loss. The untimely death of Princess Diana in 1997 will amply demonstrate the universality of this sense of belonging with an astounding outpouring of emotion from thousands who never knew her personally.

These untimely deaths are symptoms, of a sort, of the failure of my generation's flirtation with the great hippy dream; the dream of universal love, of freedom to be whatever you wish, of an end to conflict, of a shared ideal. In the end the dream betrays us; it all turns out to be ephemeral, a phase; and the world returns inexorably to its default state of selfishness, greed, prejudice, and war.

Some of the London lads have got together to play and sing (mostly Irish) folk songs. I soon become caught up in this. Although I don't have a great voice, it's OK. What I *can* do, is harmonize. Integrated into the "band," I persuade them to widen their repertoire and incorporate some English songs, traditional and contemporary. It's a natural progression to bring Cherry in. As soon as they hear her, they are as entranced as I am. Two other female friends turn out to also have lovely voices, and soon we find ourselves singing in our local pub, and invited to perform at school socials and other small events.

It's the Nook Band all over again!

In more ways than one...

Just as the Nook Band, we stroll down the path of not really going anywhere. There are strong personalities, and although the final result is always good, it is very often a fierce battle to get

History of a Daft A'porth

there. It's also difficult to rehearse often enough; people have other commitments, work, etc. Although we try hard to keep it going, eventually, just as things did in Sheffield, though this time without acrimony or 'divorce', it fizzles out. It's a pity. We weren't bad!

Cherry and I are having problems. Although in most ways very compatible: home, music, walking, friends, holidays etc, we're far apart in others. I still smoke occasionally, but it is almost always when we're out at the pub, or at a party, and I'm finding it more and more difficult to cope with her much heavier habit. She's a regular smoker. Her car ashtray is constantly full to overflowing, and the smell in the car is barely tolerable. She finds it hard to adhere to my request not to smoke in the flat and in my car. I begin to resent the odour of cigarettes on her more and more.

And she wants to have a baby.

I do not.

I'm not ready for that kind of responsibility. Nor do I wish to accept the restrictions and fears that parenthood brings. We didn't discuss the possibility of children when we first got together, (who does?) so are now broaching the subject with unfolding and diverging predispositions.

The fissures begin to widen. We're spending more time away from each other; sometimes, instead of holidays together one of us will go away for a few days on a break somewhere – she to her parents in Ireland, I to walk in Wales or the Lakes.

It can't go on. I plead with her to give up smoking. She strives to persuade me to become a father.

We stagger on like this for another few months, and finally she announces she can't take any more, and that she's leaving me. Despite the problems between us, I still love her, and this is devastating for me. I beg her to reconsider, but her mind is made up, and I hear from her lips that famous line we all know so well from the movies... that she still cares for me a great deal, but she doesn't love me any more. It's the end. I move out of the flat, and she organises the sale and division of the proceeds. Mark, one of my pub mates, generously offers me his spare room, and I gratefully, if morosely, move in.

The separation hits me hard. Breaking up with Viv left me sad and distraught, but this is much worse. Viv and I had lived together, yes, but Cherry and I were – in a phrase implying so much more – building a life together. I'm broken. I spend a lot of time crying, or pathetically begging my friends to intervene on my behalf. I still go out with them to the pub, but I'm miserable company: withdrawn, whining, and inconsolable. Steadfastly, they put up with it, to a point, at least. Eventually the murmurs of sympathy and condolence give way to suggestions for recovery, and gently couched (or not!) forms of the 'pull yourself together and get on with life' variety. Wallowing in what must become irritatingly indulgent self-pity, it takes me months to get over the split. Thankfully, despite my terminal moping, my long-suffering friends stick by me. And sharing a flat, Mark and I become very close. Unlike my previous flat shares, we live almost like a couple, dividing groceries and chores, going to the pub together to meet the crowd, watching TV together. We endure life's ordinary little indignities and pressures with mutual sympathy. Very occasionally, there's a more significant event to contend with.

One morning we come out of the flat to find whole trees strewn across the roads after what turns out to have been the biggest storm in recorded history. Forests have been flattened in swathes across the country. The previous night, Michael Fish, the TV weatherman, had assured us that "there will be no hurricane." He was so disastrously wrong, his name will become forever synonymous with erroneous predictions. Fifteen million trees have been blown down; eighteen people have lost their lives in the devastation. Slightly stunned by the extent of the catastrophe, Mark and I take the day off work (we can't get there, anyway), and laze about like teenagers while the debris is cleared outside and across the whole of southern England. The country takes weeks to recover, and Michael Fish is pilloried and mocked in the media for years.

History of a Daft A'porth

Mark is a robust and jolly fellow Yorkshireman, and possibly the kindest person I've ever met. His tolerance of my despair is boundless – thankfully – as we are in such constant proximity. I benefit from his generosity in both living-space and friendship for six long months, until I finally get myself back together, find a flat I can afford to buy, and move out of his spare room. He's saved me, and I love him dearly. Everybody loves Mark.

But the universe does not discriminate in favour of the good. Unbelievably; appallingly; three years later, Mark too becomes one of our lost heroes. On holiday somewhere exotic, far from rapid medical help, he is precipitously and ruthlessly taken from us by a sudden heart attack. He's always been overweight and a heavy drinker and smoker, and it has finally claimed him.

I receive the news, stupefied. I can't believe it. Only the week previously, I was drinking in the pub with him. It's impossible to accept the reality of his death. For the next week, I just feel numb. Incomprehension persists over the following week: the day of his funeral comes around. It's to be in Beverley, his home town, not far from Hull. We, the London friends, drive up there in various vehicles, arriving outside the small family church as the other mourners are trickling in. Respectfully, we hold back until the family and their close ones have gone in. As the last of them enter, and we begin to follow, the hearse arrives. Mark was a big man. He was a good few inches taller than most of us, broad, barrel-chested and beer-bellied, his imposing presence softened by his gentle warmth and ready laugh. So, as the bearers slide the coffin from the hearse, hoist it onto their shoulders, and begin to carry it into the church, I stare at it in confusion.

It looks so...small. So... *not enough*...

Grief hits me like a fist in the solar plexus. I've been numb and unable to accept his death before now, but the sight of that casket, seeming so hopelessly inadequate for his large frame and his expansive joie-de-vivre, make it suddenly and cruelly real. Tides of sobs sweep over me. Incapable of following the coffin into the church, I wobble to a bench in the cemetery, and sit, weeping as helplessly as I did for the children of Aberfan, until my friend Gary gently scoops me up after the service and guides me back to the car. Once again, I'm forced by this flood of pent up sorrow to weigh up how emotionally damaging my childhood may have been. Not once, when close relatives die – my grandparents, my father, my mother – am I bereft by the loss. Do I subconsciously blame the lot of them for my unhappy youth? A Hamlet complex? It's not until many years later that I'll consider the possibility that, because of my unhappy childhood, I deferred forming the normal early-attachment bonds, and transferred them as an adult to my friends and partners. Despite studying these very theories in my psychology course, I'll remain substantially blind to their implications for myself until I have children of my own. Now, though, I'm just grateful in a dark, desolate sort of way, that I *am* able to feel the crushing grief that comes with the death of someone truly loved: Mark.

History of a Daft A'porth

Chapter 14: On the Hill

There's no such thing as bad weather, only unsuitable clothing
Alfred Wainwright, A Coast to Coast Walk

We return to London, and as it must, life goes on. Mark's loss has left a huge empty space in our tight group of friends, and it will take a long time for us to find anything resembling the cheeriness and bonhomie he brought to our gatherings. In a poignant way, his death has shown up the smallness of the world we inhabit in this vast city. We're so insulated here, despite the occasional visit to far-away friends, or foreign holidays. After six years in London, I'm starting to feel a little cooped up, to miss the freedom of the easily accessible countryside that I took so much for granted as a child and in Sheffield, and I'm becoming more and more aware of its place in my life; how leaving it behind has diminished my sense of freedom.
As a small child, I first began to explore the woods, fields, and waterways of Herefordshire, Shropshire, Gloucester, and Radnorshire (a Welsh county that no longer exists), and from the start, I was at home in the outdoor world. More than at home, I felt a part of it. Even when quite young – four or five – I would extend my exploration of our surroundings far and wide, often to my mother's disquiet, and come home late for tea (which is what we Yorkshire tykes called dinner back then); tired, often grubby, but satisfied with the day's adventures. This love of the outside, bred in part from an attempt to get away from Fred's presence, gradually became a need, and from very early on, long treks grew to be an essential part of my life. When we moved back to Halifax, there were more winding, woody, country paths to discover, steep tussocky hills to climb, overgrown streams with tunnel-like covered culverts, and even an abandoned mineshaft, into which my schoolfriend David and I ventured a few paces until the thickening dark scared us out!
The distances I covered in these sallies grew longer, and when I learned to ride a bike, (quite late, around the age of ten), I added neighbouring towns to my list of conquests, gritty, grey mill-

towns with names deeply rooted in the region's Anglo-Saxon past: Heckmondwike, Mytholmroyd, Brighouse. These were very unlike the small country market-towns of the western counties that I had been used to. Sometimes I covered twenty or thirty miles there and back. Most of this was on fairly busy roads, without a helmet, and before the cycling proficiency test was even thought of. I took no particular care of my bike at first, and was shaken out of my skin one day, when, hurtling down a slope on the Bradford road towards busy traffic lights, I applied my brakes suddenly and hard, to be rewarded by my two wrongly-mounted rear brake blocks whizzing past my ears. With my heart in my mouth, I careered helplessly through the red light, only coming to a stop a hundred meters further on where the road began to slope up again. Breathing heavily, shaking like a whole tree full of leaves, and with my heart raging, I swore to do everything I could never to have to live through such a scare again. It precipitated, I believe, my drive to know how to fix things. This desire – and my apparent ability to master most of the necessary skills – I later assume I must get from my biological father, he being an engineer. From then on, any vehicle I might have would be maintained in the best condition my skills at the time could manage. Starting with my bike, which – with the help of several library books on bicycle maintenance – underwent a thorough overhaul. No more catapulted brake blocks!

Occasionally, before Ian's birth, as a family we would go on an outing to 'the country' on Fred's motorcycle, with me in the sidecar; or subsequently, on the bus or train. When we lived further south, it was the Welsh hills. From Halifax, we would go into the Yorkshire dales. I was equally entranced by each of these expanses of semi-wilderness, and took lustily to the long distances involved. These excursions are some of the few moments when being in Fred's company wasn't as onerous as usual. Perhaps it was because he felt less need to control, perhaps because I had more freedom to be myself, I don't know – but it was bearable out there, and my attachment to the landscape blossomed.

History of a Daft A'porth

While I was still at school, my wanderlust was restricted to the areas around the hamlet where we lived, then briefly around Cleckheaton after we moved there.
It's only when I come to live in Sheffield, to go to university, that my hiking horizons are really opened up.
Sheffield city is built on a series of hills surrounding the river Don valley. The city is neighbour to the industrial towns of Rotherham, Worksop, and Doncaster to the east, and borders on the Derbyshire peaks and dales in the west. The Nook is in the western half of the city, and those of us so inclined quickly discover how easily we can get out into the gentle rolling peaks of Derbyshire. It's a revelation. So much space; so much green. Mile upon mile of rolling crags and millstone outcrops. We begin to make regular trips out there whenever the weather's good and we have the time. If one is available, and suitably compliant, we drag along a friend who has a car. If I go alone, or with just one other, it's often on my motorbike. Occasionally we hitch-hike there and back (the main road from Sheffield to Manchester – the Snake Pass – runs through our favourite area). If feeling sturdy enough, on the occasions of exceptionally fine weather, we can walk all the way out and back in a day. The scenery's gorgeous; rolling heathland with rocky buttresses giving way to sinuous valleys, such as those cradling the vast Ladybower and Derwent reservoirs, as well as many smaller stretches of water. There are escarpments to climb, and wooded dales in which thousands of streams of all sizes and characters cascade their way down the valleys. Lots of small villages dot the landscape, but two become our favourites; Hope and Hathersage. Hope is often favoured, not only because it's a pretty little place, but also because it represents a kind of daily travel limit for us if we want to get comfortably back before dark. Limiting ourselves to Hope allows us to get in a good walk, have a cuppa, and be home in reasonable time. We do, of course, explore much further afield, particularly when we have the luxury of a vehicle, but Hope retains its unique, unspoken, terminus quality. Top of the list though, for me and all my close friends, is Hathersage. Hathersage is where we most often come for tea and cake after

walking the peaks. The Cosy Cottage Tea Rooms is the place to be, with its big china teapots, and its slabs of cake massive enough to rival the abandoned blocks of millstone grit that litter the surrounding valleys. Many a glorious late afternoon is spent here with good friends or a girl I'm trying to woo, and to my mind it more than equals lazing on an Oxbridge college lawn, or punting down the Thames. Sitting outside the café, with the blue ridges of the Peak district rolling away from our very feet; could it be better?

Well, yes, it could. Paradoxically, it takes the move from Sheffield to the capital for me to discover just what. It's only after moving to London, a place where just getting to the edge of the city can involve half a day's journey, and where, after six years as an inner-city denizen, I begin to suffer the claustrophobia of metropolis life, that I unexpectedly discover what the rest of the British Isles has to offer someone with a decent pair of walking boots, a set of maps and a compass.

Although I count dancing among one of my most rewarding passions, and it will continue to fill many hours, days, and even weeks, of my life with enormous joy, it's the slower but no less strenuous pursuit of hill-walking that gives me perhaps my most spiritual experiences, and which has the power to remove me almost entirely from the mundanity and occasional oppression of the world. It's out walking, at the top of some hard-won snowy peak, watching the sun begin to set over a Scottish loch, that I'll come nearest to the nirvana mentioned in many of the texts I've read in pursuit of the meaning of life, which I have never attained. Unless of course, it really is just 42.

But how does all this extra horizon stretching get under way? My friend John steps onto the stage once again! Our not infrequent visits to the pub are occasionally to see a band. One of the local ones is called Crannog; they play a regular gig at the Queen's Head in Hornsey, a ten-minute walk away from our flat. Crannog are an Irish electric folk band with a superb lead singer, and a fiddle player of exceptional dexterity. They have a loyal following in the area; their gigs are always packed. At one of these, John, who's a very sociable bloke, gets talking to a chap

History of a Daft A'porth

buying drinks at the bar. Austin, as he turns out to be, is sporting an enormous plaster cast on his leg and leaning on a crutch. John courteously offers to help carry his drinks back to his friends. I watch as a lively conversation ensues, and shortly I'm waved over to join the group. Thus begins my friendship, first with the half a dozen people in this pub, and subsequently expanding like the universe just after the big bang to include the whole of their friendship network across north London and beyond. The core group went to school and have grown up together, and are as close and symbiotic as siblings, but they are to a soul, open and welcoming. They'll become my social life and support, my fellow wild-party goers, my cricketing team-mates, my shoulders to cry on, and friends I will hold dear long after I finally leave London.

Some of these pals go with me to Stroud, to John's birthday bash. They all lived in the same area growing up, and have been going away together on holiday in various combinations since their teens. It seems I've been adopted as one of their own, as one day, they invite me to come with them. They're going to the Lake district, a place they've visited several times, to "get up a few hills." I'm happy to join them.

Up until now, the highest point I've climbed has been the four-hundred-and-thirty-five-metre-high Win Hill rising above the Ladybower reservoir and dam in Derbyshire – the training location for the famous (or infamous, depending on your point of view) Dam Buster squadron in 1943. To reach its peak, you already start from fairly high above sea level, so it's not a huge challenge. The Lake district will offer far more demanding climbs.

We set off in a couple of vehicles, stopping off at Cartmel in Cumbria to visit some relatives of one of the party, where we pass a wild night celebrating the reunion and drinking enormous quantities of the local brew. More than a little the worse for wear, we set off again for our rented cottage in Keswick the following day. First priorities are, naturally, to get groceries in for the stay and to find the local hostelry. Fully recovered from the excesses of the previous night, the group's primary task of the first evening is christening the newbie – me; once again involving copious amounts of beer followed by a local malt...or two... The following morning – again not that early, for obvious reasons – our first sallie into the peaks is to take on Great Gable. This is nine hundred and fifty metres above sea level, and you have to climb around seven hundred and fifty metres of that. It's also a long walk-in before the ascent, and of course, a long walk back. This is a far more gruelling prospect than my treks in the Derbyshire hills. But we're young and fit, and game for it.

It's worth the effort. And it *is* an effort. Unusually for the Lake District, though, the weather's fine, and the views magnificent. As it is from many a peak, the whole region is laid out before you, and on a really clear day, you can see as far as the west coast, the sea glinting beyond it: as we can on this day. It's a fine baptism of fire, and boy, do I want more! We spend a long weekend in our self-catering cottage, rising and breakfasting early to get out 'on the hill,' braving rather less clement weather, but nonetheless conquering two other classic walks: Helvellyn, and the toughest and highest in the Lakes – Sca Fell Pike. Both are 'Munros,' or more accurately, 'Furth Munros.' A Munro (named after Sir Hugo Munro, 4th Baronet, who first compiled the list in 1891), is a Scottish mountain over three thousand feet. The Furth Munros are mountains above that height in the rest of the British Isles. As most climbers just drop the "Furth," I can say I've scaled my first Munros. My first official one – Ben Nevis – is a year away. Sassenach mountains or not, they make their presence felt for the next few days in my calves! We probably all overdid it just a tad, given the relatively sedentary life we lead by comparison day to day in the big smoke. Achy muscles or not, this has had a prodigious effect on me. The grandeur and isolation of those hills, with the companionship cemented facing challenging climbs and hostile elements has hooked me, reeled me in, and hauled me gasping and full of wonder into its net.

From now on mountains will drag me away from my life in the city like iron filings to a magnet. Because it's a drive of hundreds of miles from London to the nearest decent hill, this can't happen very often, but whenever the chance arises to get away

History of a Daft A'porth

with a couple or more of my fellow addicts, we drive that drive. It's usually the Lakes, (occasionally Snowdonia) with their dark brooding peaks, beautiful and arduous all of them, that we revisit many times, armed with much thumbed copies of Alfred Wainwright's exquisitely illustrated guides, getting used to the mountains' idiosyncrasies, and becoming familiar with the many paths that snake up and down their spectacular slopes. So much so, that for some much-loved routes we've no need any more of map and compass, on well-trodden walks, these stay tucked away in rucksacks underneath boxes of sandwiches and flasks of hot tea. Over the years we climb all the well-known peaks: Skiddaw, Broad Stand (famously scaled by Coleridge, who was one of the first, apart from local farmers, to stand on the top of Scafell), Blencathra, The Langdale Horseshoe, and dozens of others: every one different, all magnificent.

Less frequently visited, because of their distance, but even more of a draw, are the Scottish mountains: for us, usually in and around Glencoe. Having been intensely moved by the beauty of the Lake district, I am even more stunned by the majesty of the Scottish peaks.

We usually go in late spring, when there's often snow, and we quickly learn from false starts and fruitless attempts at these looming and far more intimidating hills, just how much more testing and dangerous they can be. In preparation for subsequent visits, we spend time perfecting our knowledge of mountain safety, equipment, and procedures. Our next outings test our hopefully improved capabilities on difficult and challenging climbs, and we eventually become seasoned and savvy in the necessary lore, able to handle ourselves on the rugged hills.

Any mountain in severe weather can kill you, and mountains beneath a blue sky and a ravishingly beautiful soft white cloak of snow are particularly treacherous. Even if the day starts fine and clear, we know to carry bad weather gear, emergency foil bags to shelter in, spare rations, torch, and whistles. Our over-jackets are deliberately bright colours to stand out against snow and rock in search and rescue situations, and for every winter trip to significant height, each of us carries crampons and ice axe; one or two of us also slung with rope. This may seem extreme, but the constant warnings published by climbing centres and mountain rescue teams are full of terrible examples of the poorly equipped, lost, injured, stranded, or frozen. Especially in the colder months, the weather can turn on a whim from clear, calm, and sunny to dark, driving, horizontal rain, or at its most ferocious – battering, blinding blizzard. Unprepared can mean dead! It's also crucial to maintain a sense of priorities, and to know when the weather is telling you to 'go back!' Pushing on blindly through unforgiving conditions out of ego or hubris can be disastrous. Stubborn and prideful: then dead!

Ben Nevis, Scotland's highest peak, is a favourite hike of ours, but also for thousands of others, suffering as it does from its own notoriety as a tourist spot. The main route from the youth hostel to the summit is a well-maintained, wide, and well-trodden path that anyone, even small children, can easily follow. It's a long slog, but unchallenging. So accessible, in fact, that in 1911, for a bet, Henry Alexander Jr, the son of Scotland's first Ford dealer, drove a Model T to the summit and back! (There's a rediscovered film of the event available to view – for free – in in the archives of the British Film Institute. It's quite a sight!). Perhaps partly because of this reputation for relatively easy access, the mountain has claimed more than its fair share of victims.

The most popular route for experienced hill walkers is around the opposite side of the mountain from the tourist track, passing Lochan Meall an t-Suidhe, commonly known as the Halfway Loch, and scrambling up the steep north west corrie and then the main ridge, Càrn Mòr Dearg, that leads to the top. In snow and ice, these are impassable without proper equipment, and once at the summit, even experienced climbers must take extreme care; the top plateau, with its precipitous drops, is deadly in poor visibility. Luckily for the more adventurous among us, winter conditions deter all but the hardiest.

History of a Daft A'porth

Usually, that is...
One day, climbing in beautiful clear blue skies, with a blanket of snow thigh-deep in places, a small party of friends and I arrive at the foot of the corrie leading to the north face of Ben Nevis. Curving away above us, the snow-covered route has already been trodden into deep troughs by earlier climbers, but we'll obviously need axes and crampons for the final near-vertical stretch, and it will be hard going. As you get to this section, the route turns south-east from the flat moorland around the lochan, and steepens its arc in a great rush to the summit – like a mathematician's carefully drawn exponential curve. At the point where the climb begins to arrow sharply upwards, we spot two distant figures coming down through the snow towards us. As they get nearer, the figures resolve into two girls around twenty, wearing light anoraks, jeans, and trainers. They have no rucksacks or equipment of any kind; not even a lunch box between them. We, sporting our Gore-Tex, our snow boots, rope, crampons, and ice axes, and each with a bulky rucksack, can do nothing but gape at them in disbelief. Our jaws drop even further when, on reaching us, one of them asks cheerfully in a charming middle-European accent, "Can you tell us the way to Fort William, please?" Fort William, the nearest town, is about ten miles away if they follow the safest route (as opposed to the snowbound moorland direction in which they were headed). This safe route is south around the other side of the mountain, then several hours trek down the snowy track to where they can join the road. How on earth have they got here? They're completely off the tourist track, and if the weather changes, they're walking suicides! Stunned by their insouciance, and polite Englishmen that we are, we offer no criticism of their inadequate preparations and their indifference to those who would have to risk their lives in rescue. We simply instruct them on the best route down the mountain. Where they were previously destined for the wild and exposed snow-filled valley to the north west of Ben Nevis, they'll now eventually get themselves safely to the main road. We watch them disappearing behind the curve of the northwest ridge, shaking our heads with incredulity for a while,

then continue our climb. Luckily for them, the weather remains fine!

The small plateau at the summit of the mountain, with its false-promise exit routes leading to hidden and precipitous drops, has been responsible for many deaths – including those of experienced climbers. During an ice climbing course one February, I cautiously haul myself up onto the mountain top's rocky table behind Tim, my guide, having climbed with him up an ice curtain into the thick cloud enveloping the peak. It's a total white-out. Visibility is less than fifty metres. It's as though we've been transported into the dense white cocoon of an alien planet's frozen atmosphere. To get down from the peak, we must navigate across the plateau from our access point – using the Glencoe Climbing Club's detailed map of the summit – to one of the safe descent points. The only way to do this securely in the white-out is to rope and pace. We tie ourselves together with around fifty metres of rope left spare between us. Then with compass and plateau map, we take a very careful bearing in the direction of the indicated exit gulley. Tim paces out fifty metres in this direction while I pay out the rope and yell directions to keep him on the bearing. He stops at the end of the rope, and only then can I move to catch him up. The same bearing is set, and the process slowly and meticulously repeated until the safe exit emerges through the impenetrable mist. It has to be done this way. You can see nothing. Only whiteness – and your partner: not doing it correctly is how people fall to their deaths. Doing it properly, on the other hand, in this frozen, all-enveloping cloud-igloo, with the constant sense of danger sharpening the senses, is at the same time unreal, consuming, and thrilling. For years after this intense experience, I will bore my climbing friends with the story, bossing them around pompously on the snowy hills with instructions on 'how to arrest a slide off an ice slope by rolling onto your ice axe in the correct manner,' or other techniques I've learnt, until their merciless and relentless mocking finally shuts me up.

History of a Daft A'porth

Even though it's not always possible when the weather closes in, I love to get to the top. This isn't simply for the sense of achievement at having "conquered" the peak – some, I climb many times over – but rather for the sense of an effort made and rewarded. And sometimes it's repaid in spectacular fashion. The peak of the Buachaille in Glencoe is achieved from the north side suddenly and unexpectedly, by rounding a small protruding buttress of rock just below the summit. Once past this, a few metres on, the mountain drops away to reveal the whole landscape beyond. We do this for the first time on a March day so crisp you could ice a cake with it. As we step past the rocky outcrop, the sun strikes us full in our faces, partially dazzling us, and momentarily preventing us from seeing the view. Then, as we breach the summit, the light suddenly and spectacularly blazes over the crumpled purple carpet of mountains to the south west that cradle Loch Etive. They stretch their arms all the way to the handful of gems that is the Atlantic Ocean glittering on the horizon. It's so beautiful, and so sudden, we are all stunned into reverent silence.

It's this kind of otherworldly experience that mountains are extraordinarily and repeatedly capable of providing. I often enjoy coastal or countryside walks with partners or friends, and find them stimulating and beautiful, but nothing can compare with the astonishing grandeur, the scale, and the surprises, with which mountains can leave you breathless and transported...

I'm climbing Jack's (or Jake's) Rake; a long narrow sloping chimney-like cleft in the massive flat front of Pavey Ark in the Lake District's Langdale Pikes. I've climbed it before, but this time I'm with my future wife, Madeleine, also an avid hill-walker. From tranquil Stickle tarn at the base of the climb, we begin the tricky scramble up the rock, slippery with persistent drizzling rain. It's miserable weather. About half way up, it turns into thick wet mist which, as we approach the top of the rake, is unmistakeably low cloud. Finally emerging from this in the last few metres of the climb, we step out onto the top of Pavey Ark into a fairy wonderland. We're above the cloud. The arc of peaks that compose the Langdale Pikes is suspended liked a miniature tropical archipelago above a soft and gently rolling white sea stretching from our feet to the visible horizon, with dazzling, totally clear blue sky above. It's like a fluffy carpet of slowly undulating foam, so dense and uniform, we feel we could step out onto it and stroll to the nearby island summits. It is truly, heart-stoppingly magical. This is what I climb for. This, and so many other breathtakingly beautiful vistas are what I spend so much effort and sweat to achieve. Climbing these and other slopes of various geologies and characters will become a minor obsession for me that will persist until unreliable older knees and a less than healthy pair of older lungs constrain my efforts to lower contours. Even then, my yearning for the high peaks, and my memories of vistas such as these will continue to fire my imagination.

History of a Daft A'porth

Chapter 15: Greasepaint: 2 – Age and Character

The theatre is so endlessly fascinating because it's so accidental. It's so much like life.

Arthur Miller

You'd think that with all this watching bands, dancing, and climbing of mountains, I'd have little time for theatre. I abandoned it as a career to take up photography, and in that, I'm now established. Work at H-studios is absorbing, and I feel sufficiently qualified and experienced to no longer suffer from imposter syndrome – in the way I did when I started off as Andy's assistant in Sheffield; or when putting in the submission for my AMPA at K- Photography. When I arrive in London, my intimate contact with theatre is maintained only by the arrangement I establish with Mountview Theatre School, taking the front-of-house pictures for their shows. Otherwise, my life in theatre is all behind me.
And then I meet Mike.

Mountview's courses for acting and technical students run for three years, and entry is by audition. But they also do a 'post-graduate' course of one year, which pretty much anyone can join as long as they stump up the fee. Students on the course are usually people in their thirties and forties who want to dip their toes in the professional world for a bit, or to improve their skills for amateur company shows. Mike is one of these. But he's been well and truly bitten by the bug. The bug that says he wants to start his own theatre company – unusually, as a producer, not an actor. He knows me, and my background in 'the business,' and one evening he buttonholes me in the bar, laying out his ideas for starting the company, hiring, rehearsing, playing in pub theatres, etc. But he's no idea what script to start off with. Do I have any suggestions? It should be small cast, low-budget set, no difficult lighting or effects etc. (His finances limit the vision!). I offer *Kennedy's Children*, by Robert Patrick. Back in Sheffield, I went to see this at the Crucible theatre, and was so moved and impressed that I ended up directing it twice myself: once with the actors in Go-Dangle, as a fund-raiser, and a year later as a guest director for the university Theatre group, with student actors. It's an exceptionally powerful and emotional play, with wonderful roles for every one of its five main cast. I give the script to Mike to assess. Two days later he accosts me again in the bar, excitement frothing out of him.

"Pete!! It's brilliant! It's fantastic! Just right!"

"Great, I'm glad."

"Will you direct it?"

"Oh come on, Mike, I've already done it twice, and I've got a full-time job."

"Please, please? Pretty please?"

Versions of his persistent pleading, and my persistent refusal, volley back and forth between us over the course of the next few days leading up to the graduation ceremonies. Mike insists he can't find anyone else he can trust or that he feels is right to do this, and that he'll arrange everything around me if I'll only agree.

I have to say, ego plays a part in this. I'm flattered by the attention and praise.

I give in. Mike is ecstatic. In his producer role, he will organise auditions, rehearsals, performances and venues, and will handle publicity.

Auditions are held in a community arts centre in Elephant and Castle.

In my view, one of the most important skills a director can possess is that of casting. I'm lucky in this respect. I seem to have a knack of casting the right people. Half the work is done for you if you have an actor who's mastered their craft. A good director can get the best from fine actors, but no amount of experience or skill can coax a great performance from a lousy actor. So I make it plain to Mike, that if we don't get people who are up to the task, the production would suffer, and we would give our audiences an inferior show. A question I always put to cast and crew is "Who's the most important individual in a theatre?" Answer: the person on a seat watching: if they're not

History of a Daft A'porth

entertained and stimulated, you're not doing your job. So casting matters. We see around a hundred young, and not-so young actors, and we're lucky enough to find five of them that shine through.

Rehearsals are long and tough. Because Mike and I both work – he drives a delivery van – they're held at evenings and weekends. There's a lot of one-to-one work for me with each actor, because in this script, the actors talk not to each other, but only to the audience; relating their loves and hates, their joys and their despairs, in a series of interspersed monologues. Done well, it's riveting.

And it seems we do it well. We perform to audiences in one or two pub theatre venues, and in the prestigious Archway Arts Centre theatre. Our show gets a mention on Capital Radio. The DJ calls it out as the best show in London! For days I can't get through a door because my head is so swollen.

Flushed, as they say, with success, Mike and I decide to continue the company, he as producer, me as artistic director. We go on to make and perform a further four shows. Sadly, none of them are as successful as *Kennedy's Children*. Our second one comes close, but we almost abandon it before it even gets off the ground. It's a trilogy called *Gimme Shelter,* from the pen of playwright Barry Keeffe, exploring failure, defiance, reconciliation and acceptance. A character we simply know as 'the kid' appears in the first and third plays. This role, particularly in the first part of the trilogy, is a peach, requiring powerful displays of despair, contempt, and rage. We've cast all the other parts, but after auditioning more than twenty actors for 'the kid,' I've seen no-one of the right playing-age – fifteen – with sufficient ability or commitment. This role is so pivotal, not using a first-rate actor in the part would let down the whole show, and I'd rather cancel than compromise. A friend who works at the arts centre where we rehearse has told us she has passed on audition details to T-, a student at Putney college. He attends the improvisation workshops she regularly runs there, and he is, she says, 'pretty good.'

"Tell him to come along," says Mike.

It's the last night of auditions, and nine o'clock has come and gone. We've seen the last auditionee for 'the kid,' and he was utterly useless. Demoralised, we've turned off the lights and are locking the door, when a skinny youth runs up, panting with exertion. He has the shaved head, Doc Martins, short-leg jeans, and the obligatory braces of an east-end skinhead.

"Hello," he manages, in a strong London accent, "Are these the auditions?"

"Well, they were," I say, "We're locking up, mate; we've just finished. You're a bit too late!"

"Oh! I'm really sorry, I'm T-, I've just got out of a class... can I please...?"

He looks so downcast, so forlorn, we give in. What the hell, it'll only take a few minutes... it's an act of charity. We open up again, and T- follows us in.

"OK, what have you got for us?"

"Er, it's a bit from a play called *Iron*. Do you mind if I use the script? I haven't had time to learn it properly."

Mike and I exchange rolled eyes. He hasn't even learned it! Another complete waste of time.

"Yes, alright, go on then..."

He begins.

Five minutes later, when he's finished, both our jaws have dropped with astonishment. A tour-de force! His delivery of the chosen speech, despite occasional glances at the text, was riveting, nuanced, moving, and mature. Amazing! There's no question, at the eleventh hour – indeed at one second to twelve – we've found our 'Kid.' It's almost a miracle.

He doesn't let us down: even if, raw and untrained, he needs help with technique and stage discipline; I teach him, for example, how not to hurt other actors in scenes involving violence. But his brilliant performance is the fulcrum of the show, and our audiences enthusiastically recognise it.

A TV producer attends one of the shows, and a few months later, T- has his first telly role. 5 years later, I watch him scuttle athletically around as Gregor, in Kafka's strange cipher of a play, *Metamorphosis,* on the stage of the Mermaid Theatre. Thirty

History of a Daft A'porth

years later he will be one of the brightest stars in the Hollywood firmament, appearing in films by Quentin Tarantino, Tom Stoppard, and Rowan Joffe, and I regard it as a small badge of honour that his first professional role – albeit a profit-share of tiny proportions – was with me and Mike. His full name: Tim Roth.

Our little theatre company, alas, does not go on to such great things. We both work hard during 'normal' hours, and then put in almost another full week's-worth of time for the shows on top of this. It's draining; and critically, after two years of hard slog, the work begins to show the strain. Our final show together does not do well. Too hurriedly, I pick an obscure play, a comedy, which just doesn't gel. Our leading actress struggles in the role, and we waste a lot of time. We don't have enough left to build a decent set, rehearsals stutter and drag, reviews and audiences are desultory. Mike and I are exhausted running a theatre company, while each holding down a full-time job. After a fairly disastrous run, neither of us can face carrying on, and we agree to call it a day. Tears are shed.

It's at times like these that many would say, 'Give it a rest!' or 'Haven't you learned anything?' or even, 'Maybe it's not for you.' And of course, some of my friends do say such things...

What they don't understand, and will never understand, however, is that for some of us theatre's not just an interest, a hobby, or even a passion, it's an addictive drug. For these people, once we've heard the roll of applause that bursts joyfully from a happy audience and washes over us like a warm Mediterranean breeze, there's no going back. Actor or director, the same need surges in you, and the same withdrawal pains afflict you as they do any addict. I can't to this day go to see a show without mentally donning my director's hat. Even if the show is superb, I'll be checking off the good and bad points of the production, and playing each role as I see it in my head; a poor performance will make me cringe in sympathy for the other members of the audience. But above all of these addiction-driven tics, it's prolonged absence from active involvement that casts me adrift in a sea of distracted longing. I miss it as I would miss a lost love.

And so – fool that I am – I go looking for my next score!

I'm committed to photography as a career now, and the painful failure of my last show with Mike has made me wary of any further extra-curricular involvement in professional theatre. The problem is though, that after a while, I begin to suffer withdrawal symptoms. Maybe I should look at joining an amateur company for my fix? My view of the amateur scene, though, is prejudiced by having worked with professionals. It would be easy to take my seeming disdain for amateur theatre as intolerable snobbery; looking down on people who enjoy their hobby immensely. I certainly don't mean it that way. Working diligently and consistently in any business with high professional standards almost inevitably imbues one to some extent with those harsh standards. Theatre's no different. Moving from the professional environment to the amateur can be a bit of a culture shock, and it's not always easy to react generously. I'm very aware that the amateur scene doesn't necessarily have the same aims. Yes, most amateurs are very committed, work as hard as any professional, and can be just as talented. For some, however, the social side comes first, theatre being more of a means to that end. Not everyone agrees with Hamlet that "The play's the thing..." This is difficult for me. I'm used to a completely different way of working. Of course actors are a social lot, but the show always comes first. I've worked with actors who have – quite literally – bled for their craft. (In *Kennedy's Children* one of the cast accidentally snapped a glass in his hand in a moment of his character's distress, dripping blood onto the stage for some minutes until his exit.) This kind of professional commitment is, inevitably, influenced by the fact that if you don't perform well, you'll get sacked. Amateurs aren't under the same pressures; it's not a career. But I've been in amateur casts where for example, someone turned up late for rehearsals because their favourite TV show was on. This isn't to say that the world of pro' theatre is superior in every way: far

History of a Daft A'porth

from it! As an audience member, I've left more than one so-called professional company's show at the interval, having endured a badly acted, and incompetently directed turkey of a show (or half of it, at least!). In many instances, amateurs outperform their professional peers in every sense of the word. There are holes in the theory, I admit.

That said, I set about researching the many amateur companies that abound in Greater London: which has the best reputation; which are more accessible; which have their own premises, etc. Turns out there are two that rate consistently highly, receiving regular good reviews, and running themselves competently and with good practices. The first, in Ealing, is rather a long way for easy rehearsal commuting; the second, in Islington, is ideal.

The Tower Theatre company has its own building, a 16th century grade-one-listed tower and house, and a full proscenium-stage, raked auditorium, changing and rehearsal rooms, props space, and bar. It's quite a sophisticated set-up; would give many small provincial theatres a good run for their money (No pun intended!). Also, entry to the acting company is only by audition – which is a good sign.

I go to see a couple of the Tower shows. They're not bad. One of them is excellent: a production of *The Accidental Death of an Anarchist* – fizzing with physicality, and very funny. I get to know a couple of the members and find out a bit more. It becomes obvious that they take theatre very seriously – but still have a lot of fun! I can't resist any longer; I audition. Good old *Kennedy's Children* provides dozens of fabulous speeches, and I pick one by Sparger. Sparger is a campily gay, off-off-Broadway actor, whose story runs from junkie teenage prostitute, through crazy improvised New York café cabaret, to tragic and bloody loss of beloved friends.

It's a good choice: I'm in.

I try out for the next production – Shaw's *Arms and the Man*, and get a part: a nice one: Bluntschli – the play's 'conscience'. It's the start of a long and vigorous relationship with The Tower, both backstage and on it.

And it's at The Tower that I will meet the woman who will change my life.

History of a Daft A'porth

Chapter 16: Last Lines: A Mad World

A true soul mate is probably the most important person you'll ever meet, because they tear down your walls and smack you awake.
Elizabeth Gilbert

1989. The Berlin Wall has fallen, the 'World-Wide-Web' has been invented, global warming has been confirmed, Margaret Thatcher has introduced the Poll Tax, Rowan Atkinson has launched Comic Relief, and I've been a member of the Tower Theatre Company for two years.

When I moved out of Mark's place, I bought a small ground-floor flat in Finsbury Park. It's a box, with two main rooms, kitchen, and bathroom, in a squat, ugly 1960s red-brick block of eight flats that fronts onto busy Tollington Park road. A rare and highly treasured bonus in London is the small car park at the back. Parking spaces are like gold-dust; so we're very fortunate. If the lease allowed us to sell it, the parking area alone could probably make us all millionaires! But it doesn't. Ah well! Expenses, management fees, etc are shared equally by the eight tenants, and although we don't mix socially, we do all get on, thank goodness. The block is in Finsbury Park: one of those busy, cosmopolitan mini-centres that make up village-London. The main road buzzes with trade for a multicultural bazaar of shops; a global display of fruit and veg in strange colours and even stranger shapes: from Turkey, Greece, India, Pakistan, and Poland; a smattering of halal butchers, ethnic restaurants, and small cafes where old men with long moustaches and loud voices hang out to smoke, violently slap down dominoes, and reminisce boisterously about each of their personal 'old countries.'

Nearby are the busy Finsbury Park tube and bus stations. The park itself is only ten minutes from my door, and if the weather's OK, I spend many hours there with a book and a long cold drink. I can walk to trendy Crouch End, where most of my pub friends hang out, in about fifteen minutes, and the drive to work in Notting Hill takes me about forty-five. I've got the route so distilled now, I would happily challenge a London cabbie to better me on it.

I can't quite afford the mortgage on my own, so I rent out one of the rooms to a girl called Sarah, who works for the local council. We get on well, but, like the other inhabitants of our four-floored little hutch, we don't socialise much. Occasionally we throw a party, but these are not frequent. Inevitably, when Sarah moves in, I have to suffer the obligatory prurient teasing from my so-called friends regarding my intentions toward my cohabitee. They persist irritatingly for a while, recalling more than a little those unimaginative taunts from childhood, when "*She's your girlfriend*" was the sophisticated height of playground slander. To my relief, my friends abandon this lost cause after a few tedious weeks.

I'm still going to ceilidhs, especially Sidmouth every August now, where I 'set up house' with John's Cotswolds crowd in the ever-more elaborate campsite village they bring with them. I too am now such a regular, that I'm on first-name terms with a few of the bands. It's my great privilege and pleasure to cut a rug in many a rocket-fuelled frenzy of a Strip-the-Willow, with such greats as Cathy Lesurf of the Oyster Band, and Blowzabella's Jo Freya, both hugely talented and versatile musicians, and both brilliant dancers of enormous energy and skill.

Work is also going well. I get on easily with clients, and I've even established closer relationships with some of them than perhaps have my employers. The pieces of the jigsaw seem to be fitting in to place. Work, theatre, dancing, pub, friends, etc.

But something's still missing...

The Tower's good reputation, I find, is well deserved. They're incredibly committed. I find out that several members have even gone on to illustrious stage careers. My first outing with them as Bluntschli was hugely enjoyable, and followed by several smaller roles, but I've thrown myself particularly into backstage life, building sets, making props, and helping with get-ins and get-outs.

History of a Daft A'porth

I've had romantic dalliances with a couple of members of the Tower since joining, and one or two short-lived relationships outside, but nothing serious. No-one quite fits the demanding and idealistic role I still have carefully stored in my head for the 'right one.' And after my experiences with Viv and Cherry, I've begun to seriously doubt the possibility of finding someone with whom I can be truly happy. I'm at least fortunate enough to have let go of past griefs, and to get on with daily life.

I've made good friends at The Tower, all really committed to making the shows as professional as possible; following the principle of the most important person in the theatre being the one who pays to watch the show. For me, this is deeply ingrained, and I admit, a bit obsessive. Sending the audience out happy (or at least fulfilled) is the ultimate aim. Everyone else involved – actors, director, crew – is simply a means to an end. It's an approach that can be demanding, I know, and I'm aware that I and my fellow obsessives can be a bit hard to take. At times this tack results in a certain hostility We're berated – usually, but not always, good-naturedly – for pushing too hard; being too perfectionist; too intent on the goal. This applies to backstage work just as much as acting. Always pushing to ensure things are 'done right,' can get up the most tolerant of noses. I try my best, therefore, to keep the tendency in check, but me being me, it's hard.

So it is one evening, when the challenge of attaching scenery to a bar some twenty feet up a ladder on the Tower stage relegates sensible restraint to the backstage area of my head. I ask my co-rigger in the task if she knows how to use a hammer properly. My motive is purely practical. Holding a hammer halfway down its shaft makes harder work than necessary. Holding it at the end is both easier and more efficient. Without tact, however, pointing this out implies the other person is a complete idiot! As soon as the words leave my big mouth, I know I should have kept it shut.

My co-rigger in this case is a petite, pretty, curly-haired blond girl in jeans, a floppy T-shirt and a jauntily-angled beret. She regards me, eyes narrowed, weighing the question. "Yes, thank you," she replies after a pause, "I do know how to use a hammer properly." She turns back to the work, and demonstrates her perfectly competent use of said hammer, driving in a series of nails with ease. "That alright for you?" she enquires with a pointed little smile.

"Er, yes. Perfect."

Her name, I discover, is Madeleine. Mad for short. In the bar, later, our backdrop-hanging successfully completed, she unsheathes a sharply bladed sense of humour, gently but ruthlessly slicing up my ladder-top pomposity, and generating raucous mirth at my expense amongst our fellow riggers. It's a merciless but good-natured filleting of my inane condescension. Thankfully, it's also – in Humphrey Bogart's words to Claude Rains at the end of the glorious *Casablanca* – the beginning of a beautiful friendship.

That I get away with it so lightly – this awkward first exchange – leaves me astonished and eternally grateful. Instead of consigning me – and I deserved it – to the ranks of complete tossers she's known and quickly forgotten, she henceforth treasures the incident as a much-visited anecdote.

Because it's a friendship that will turn into a love affair, and evolve into a relationship still strong thirty-odd years later when I write these last few lines.

It won't be smooth. In fact, it will be turbulent. It will teeter precariously on the brink more than once, tearfully brought back from the edge each time. There'll be joy and there'll be tragedy. We won't always sing in harmony, but over the years Mad's kindness, patience, love and forgiveness will eventually help me become – despite my constant flaws and my resistance to change – a better man. We will have two wonderful daughters; each birth, each new person, their own unique and fascinating story.

We will leave London and set up home in Bath.

I will change careers a further three times.

And after twenty-eight years together, Mad and I will finally tie the knot.

But most important of all; the hardships and the setbacks, the disappointments and the tears accepted, our life together will

History of a Daft A'porth

triumph over all that, to be filled with, and surrounded by love. After all the years of fear, anxiety, and loneliness, that scared little boy from Halifax will finally pull his head out of the armchair cushions, look around himself with wide-open eyes, and realise at last just how lucky he is.
It's the beginning, not just of another chapter, but of a whole new story.

But that – as better authors than I have often promised – is for another day.

And no, she will never let me forget that hammer...

21 September 2021

Printed in Great Britain
by Amazon